SO-ABB-228

Social Issues
in Literature

Women's Search for Independence in Charlotte Brontë's *Jane Eyre*

Other Books in the Social Issues in Literature Series:

Social Issues in Literature

Women's Search for Independence in Charlotte Brontë's *Jane Eyre*

Claudia Durst Johnson, Book Editor

GREENHAVEN PRESS
A part of Gale, Cengage Learning

GALE
CENGAGE Learning

Detroit • New York • San Francisco • New Haven, Conn • Waterville, Maine • London

Christine Nasso, *Publisher*
Elizabeth Des Chenes, *Managing Editor*

© 2011 Greenhaven Press, a part of Gale, Cengage Learning

Gale and Greenhaven Press are registered trademarks used herein under license.

For more information, contact:
Greenhaven Press
27500 Drake Rd.
Farmington Hills, MI 48331-3535
Or you can visit our Internet site at gale.cengage.com

For product information and technology assistance, contact us at

Gale Customer Support, 1-800-877-4253
For permission to use material from this text or product, submit all requests online at www.cengage.com/permissions

Further permissions questions can be emailed to permissionrequest@cengage.com

Articles in Greenhaven Press anthologies are often edited for length to meet page requirements. In addition, original titles of these works are changed to clearly present the main thesis and to explicitly indicate the author's opinion. Every effort is made to ensure that Greenhaven Press accurately reflects the original intent of the authors. Every effort has been made to trace the owners of copyrighted material.

Cover photograph copyright © David Lyons/Alamy.

LIBRARY OF CONGRESS CATALOGING-IN-PUBLICATION DATA

Women's search for independence in Charlotte Brontë's Jane Eyre / Claudia Durst Johnson, Book Editor.
    p. cm. -- (Social issues in literature)
    Includes bibliographical references and index.
    ISBN 978-0-7377-5450-6 (hardcover) -- ISBN 978-0-7377-5451-3 (pbk.)
    1. Brontë, Charlotte, 1816-1855. Jane Eyre. 2. Women's rights in literature. 3. Governesses in literature. I. Johnson, Claudia Durst, 1938-
    PR4167.J5W66 2011
    823'.8--dc22
                                                            2010043626

Printed in the United States of America
1 2 3 4 5 6 7 15 14 13 12 11

Contents

Chapter 1: Background on Charlotte Brontë

   Charlotte Brontë was reared in Haworth, England, attended boarding school, worked as a governess, went to study abroad, and returned to Haworth to become a novelist.

   Lowood School in *Jane Eyre* was universally recognized as Cowan Bridge School, which the four Brontë girls attended, two of them dying from conditions there.

Chapter 2: *Jane Eyre* and Woman's Search for Independence

   In the course of Jane's rebellious pursuit of economic and inner independence, she trades in the traditional religion of the patriarchy for an Earth Mother.

   Unlike the subjugated women of her day, Jane Eyre develops her own independent vision, incorporating it into her autobiography.

Chapter 3: Contemporary Perspectives on Female Independence

Introduction

When Charlotte Brontë published her most famous novel, *Jane Eyre*, in 1847, she was labeled a dangerous, furious woman who had written a book that could rend the social fabric beyond repair. Still, it was an immediate popular success and has continued to be one of the most enduring novels in English literature.

There is no question among critics that the major theme of Brontë's novel is Jane's quest for independence. There is also little question that Jane's journey to selfhood takes her through hostile territory at a dishonorable period in English history. Three contextual issues that worked against a woman's independence are raised by Brontë: British colonialism, rigidly maintained class barriers, and social attitudes toward women.

The frequent mentions of the British Empire in *Jane Eyre* create parallels between Jane's lowly dependency and colonies overpowered and ruled by England. These countries or areas were taken over and developed by the English for business reasons, primarily to have access to the colonies' natural resources and labor, to use the countries to England's advantage in time of war, and to convert the natives to Christianity. The countries colonized by England during the early years of the nineteenth century, when *Jane Eyre* is set, included the Falklands, Sierra Leone, Australia, New Zealand, India, Grenada, South Africa, Canada, Egypt, Hong Kong, and Jamaica. For the most part, the populations in these countries provided slave labor, and decisions regarding them were made by the British government. The first mention of a colony in *Jane Eyre* is Jamaica, where, the reader learns early on, Jane's uncle has gone to make his fortune. It is also the home of Bertha and her brother, presumably upper-class natives who collaborated with their British conquerors. Furthermore, Rochester makes his fortune there by marrying Bertha before he comes into his inheritance. And, of course, Jane's own economic independence is made possible by her uncle's business in Jamaica. Jamaica had been seized by the British in 1655 and continued to be ruled by the British until 1962. In 1831, sixteen years before the publication of *Jane Eyre*, an important rebellion was raised by Jamaicans to gain their independence.

The subject of colonialism arises when St. John Rivers decides to become a missionary to India, which was also ruled by Britain and would not gain its independence until the mid-twentieth century. When Jane considers his forceful command to come with him, she sees that such an action would kill her.

Another contextual social issue, raised by Jane's journey toward independence, is that of the British class system in the nineteenth century. The novel is set during a time when English royalty still stood firmly and alone at the top of the social ladder. Slightly beneath the royalty came the landed gentry, the class to which Rochester and his friends belong. A gradually softening divide existed between the landed gentry and the new, wealthy upper middle class with its successful factory owners. Jane's position in the lower middle class is determined by the clerical rank of her father, the upper-middle-class rank of her mother, and her formal education. She knows even as a child that her assignment to this rank is despised by her "betters" such as the Reeds. Her poverty and the necessity that she make her own living consigns her to the only work available to an educated woman—that of governess—even though it leaves her unsatisfied and makes her feel trapped, like a servant, at the beck and call of a master. She feels her dependent position when Rochester does the unthinkable and forces her to attend a party for his upper-class friends, who openly humiliate her. The subject of rank arises again when Jane and Rochester do the unthinkable and marry each other across class lines.

The third issue directly related to Jane's dependency is the view of women in the nineteenth century. Despite England's having had a powerful female monarch—Elizabeth I—in its history and despite the long reign of Queen Victoria beginning in 1837, women of every class were regarded as weak temptresses. Woman was still Eve, easily tempted herself and inclined to corrupt others. It was thus necessary for her to be controlled by men—to be kept dependent on men, economically, socially, and psychologically. A good woman's true profession was to be a wife and mother, confined to the house and church. Poor women, of course, could not be good women because they had, of necessity, to be tainted by hard, dirty work in the Industrial Revolution. In either case, women were ruled by their fathers, brothers, husbands, masters, and, often, their sons. Educated single women, like Jane, were locked out of professions and businesses. Even in her schoolteaching, Jane is ruled totally by St. John Rivers.

Of course, Jane is not just struggling for social and economic independence; she wants the psychological independence to form her own opinions, speak her own mind, make her own choices, feel her own worth, and affirm who she is.

The following selections begin with a section on biography that shows the similarities between Charlotte Brontë's experience and Jane Eyre's. The longer second section consists of literary criticism. Although the great body of criticism recognizes that the main theme of the novel is Jane's struggle for independence, there has been no consensus on whether and how she achieves it, the definition of independence, the price Jane and others pay for her independence, nor the form that that independence takes.

Typically, critics have assumed that in the end Jane has achieved her independence, perhaps even forming a matriarchy. Some critics enlarge on Jane's fight against social conventions and organized religion in the course of her struggle. Others write of the place her sexual awakening has in her self-fulfillment and the necessity to control her own passion. Some critics take the minority view that, despite her rebelliousness,

Jane is essentially socially conservative. A growing number disagree with Jane's view of her independence after she marries Rochester. Romance, they argue, is simply not compatible with selfhood.

The last section of the book is devoted to women's quest for independence today and what impedes that quest in the twenty-first century.

Chronology

1814
Charlotte's sister Maria is born.

1815
Charlotte's sister Elizabeth is born.

April 21, 1816
Charlotte Brontë is born.

1817
Charlotte's brother, Patrick Branwell, is born.

1818
Emily Brontë is born.

1820
Charlotte's sister Anne is born.

1821
Charlotte's mother dies of tuberculosis. Her mother's sister, Elizabeth Branwell, moves into the Brontë's home in Haworth, where their father is a rector.

1824
Maria and Elizabeth are sent to Cowan Bridge School for the daughters of clergymen. Later, Charlotte and Emily are sent there.

1825
Elizabeth and Maria die of tuberculosis. Charlotte and Emily return home from Cowan Bridge School.

1831
Charlotte attends Roe Head School.

1835

Charlotte teaches at Roe Head School, where Emily is a student. Branwell, an alcoholic and drug addict, attempts to make a grand entrance into the London art world but never even reaches the Royal Academy, returning home shortly after he arrived.

1841

Charlotte is a governess for the White family.

1842

Emily and Charlotte go to Brussels for an education that will prepare them to open their own school. Their Aunt Branwell, who had reared them, dies.

1843

Charlotte receives her diploma for the Pensionnat at Brussels, and Emily returns home.

1844

Charlotte returns from Brussels, where she had been teaching. Her and Emily's attempt to start a private school fails.

1846

A book of poems by the three sisters is published using pseudonyms.

1847

Charlotte's novel *The Professor* is rejected by the publisher. Anne's *Agnes Grey* and Emily's *Wuthering Heights* are published. *Jane Eyre* is published under the name of Currer Bell.

1848

Emily and Anne die of tuberculosis. Branwell, a gifted artist who lived a dissolute life, dies of tuberculosis.

1849

Shirley is published.

1853

Villette is published.

1853

Novelist Elizabeth Gaskell visits Charlotte.

1854

Charlotte marries Arthur Bell Nicholls.

1855

Charlotte discovers she is pregnant. She dies at the age of thirty-eight from tuberculosis and complications of pregnancy.

1857

Charlotte's *The Professor* is published. Elizabeth Gaskell's biography of Charlotte is published.

Background on
Charlotte Brontë

The Fight for Independence as Student, Governess and Writer

Herbert J. Rosengarten

Herbert J. Rosengarten, a professor and former head of the Department of English at the University of British Columbia, has edited numerous books on fiction and written several articles on the Brontës and Jane Eyre.

Charlotte Brontë, the daughter of a clergyman, grew up in the isolated and unhealthy Yorkshire village of Haworth. One of the greatest influences on her life was her relationship with her brother and four sisters, who became absorbed in the fantasy kingdoms they created together. The girls, including Charlotte, were sent to a boarding school for clergymen's daughters. The abominable conditions there, which cost the lives of two of her sisters, form a prominent part of Jane Eyre. *After Charlotte's failure as a governess, she and her sister Emily decided to open their own school after seeking training in language in Brussels. There she fell in love with the married man who appears in her novels. But the school they established failed, and Charlotte turned to writing (four novels and a book of poetry) in further pursuit of economic independence. After turning down several proposals of marriage, she finally accepted that of the Reverend Arthur Bell Nicholls but died in childbirth the year after they married.*

Charlotte Brontë's fame and influence rest on a very slender canon of published works: only four novels and some contributions to a volume of poetry. Her reputation may be explained in part by the astounding success of her first novel,

Jane Eyre; it owes much also to the romantic appeal of her personal history, given prominence soon after her death by Elizabeth Cleghorn Gaskell's excellent biography, a work preeminent in its genre. Of greater importance, perhaps, is the recognition by historians of fiction that Charlotte Brontë's work made a significant contribution to the development of the novel; her explorations of emotional repression and the feminine psyche introduced a new depth and intensity to the study of character and motive in fiction, anticipating in some respects the work of such writers as George Eliot and D.H. Lawrence.

Brontë in a Society That Exploits Women's Dependence

Her strength as a novelist lies in her ability to portray in moving detail the inner struggles of women who are endowed with a powerful capacity for feeling, yet whose social circumstances deny them the opportunity for intellectual or emotional fulfillment. Charlotte Brontë was not in any formal sense a proponent of women's rights, but in her writing she speaks out strongly against the injustices suffered by women in a society that restricts their freedom of action and exploits their dependent status. Her protests grew out of her own experience, which provided much of the material for her fiction; though she once insisted that "we only suffer reality to *suggest*, never to *dictate*," her novels include many characters and incidents recognizably drawn from her life, and her heroines have much in common with their creator.

Charlotte Brontë was born on 21 April 1816 at Thornton in the West Riding of Yorkshire. Her father, Patrick Brontë, a native of County Down in Ireland, had risen above the poverty of his family to become an undergraduate at St. John's College, Cambridge, and in 1807 was ordained a priest in the Church of England. In 1812 he met, courted, and married Maria Branwell, a pious and educated young woman from

Cornwall. Their life together was tragically brief; Maria bore six children in seven years. . . . Her death may have been hastened by the family's move in 1820 from Thornton to Haworth, where Mr. Brontë had been appointed perpetual curate. . . . Sanitation in Haworth was primitive: as late as 1850 a government inspector found open sewers and overflowing cesspits on the main street, next to outlets for drinking water. It is hardly surprising that infant mortality rates in Haworth were high or that there were frequent outbreaks of cholera and typhoid. Throughout her life, Charlotte Brontë was to suffer from fevers, colds, and bilious attacks undoubtedly attributable to this most inhospitable environment.

Nor was there much consolation to be found in the society of Haworth. Its inhabitants, even thirty years later, struck Mrs. Gaskell as a "wild, rough population" among whom there was "little display of any of the amenities of life." Mr. Brontë won the respect of his parishioners, but there was little social contact between the townsfolk and the family at the parsonage; the Brontë children thus turned to one another for companionship and entertainment. . . .

School of Death

In August 1824 Mr. Brontë sent Charlotte to join Maria and Elizabeth at the recently opened Clergy Daughters' School at Cowan Bridge, near Tunstall in Lancashire. This was a charitable institution, where the daughters of poor clergymen might receive an education suited to their station and be prepared for future employment as governesses. Its founder was William Carus Wilson, a well-intentioned but overzealous clergyman who appears to have given little thought to the physical needs of the children in his charge; he imposed a stern regime of ascetic piety and self-denial which, in combination with inadequate attention to proper diet and the unhealthy situation of the school buildings, produced a succession of illnesses among the pupils and an outbreak of typhoid in April

1825. . . . Her own sisters were among the victims of such conditions: first Maria, then Elizabeth, contracted consumption, were removed from the school, and died at home, Maria on 6 May 1825 and her sister on 15 June 1825. The death of Maria was especially painful to Charlotte; her eldest sister had become a guide and mentor, and Charlotte would later eulogize her patient virtue and premature wisdom in *Jane Eyre* in the portrait of Helen Burns.

After this tragic loss, Mr. Brontë decided to educate his children himself, and for the next six years they lived at home under the watchful eyes of Aunt Branwell and Tabitha Ackroyd, the parsonage servant. . . .

Childhood Tales

Their apprenticeship to literature had begun before the deaths of Maria and Elizabeth with the composition and performance of little plays under Maria's direction. After the return from Cowan Bridge, Charlotte and Branwell assumed the leadership in devising imaginary worlds populated by romantic figures from myth, history, and high society, whose doings they chronicled in a series of interwoven tales. . . . That a group of imaginative children should collaborate in the creation of a fantasy world is by no means unusual; what sets the storymaking of the youthful Brontës apart is that it occupied them all well into adulthood. . . .

Roe Head School

[In 1831] she was sent to Roe Head, a small private school near Mirfield under the direction of Miss Margaret Wooler and her sisters. Here she stayed for a year and a half in much happier circumstances than at Cowan Bridge; indeed, Miss Wooler was to become a lifelong friend, and Brontë would return to Roe Head in 1835 as an assistant teacher. . . .

At Roe Head, Charlotte worked hard to make up for the deficiencies in her formal education; Ellen Nussey later recalled that she "always seemed to feel that a deep responsibility rested upon her; that she was an object of expense to those at home, and that she must use every moment to attain the purpose for which she was sent to school, i.e., to fit herself for governess life. . . ."

Charlotte as Governess

Anne's departure from Miss Wooler's school in December 1837, and her own increasingly depressed spirits, led Charlotte to give up her post and return to Haworth in May 1838. Her respite was brief, however; the family's precarious financial circumstances, made more difficult by Branwell's failure to establish himself as a painter in Bradford, led Charlotte Brontë to seek employment once again, and in May 1839 she became governess to the children of the Sidgwick family of Stonegappe, near Lothersdale. The experience was an unhappy one: the Sidgwicks treated Brontë with what seemed to her to be undue coldness and condescension; the children tormented her by their rudeness and lack of discipline; and after less than three months she was back at home, telling Ellen Nussey that "I never was so glad to get out of a house in my life." . . .

Under the pressure of "proper duties," Brontë left home once again in March 1841 to become a governess in the White family at Rawdon, near Bradford. The Whites proved to be more amiable employers than the Sidgwicks; but Brontë left them in December to set in motion a plan the family had discussed for six months. This was for the three sisters to open their own school, with financial support from Aunt Branwell; as a preliminary step to strengthen their qualifications for such a venture, Charlotte and Emily wanted to spend a half-year in school on the Continent, where they might improve their grasp of foreign languages. Belgium was fixed upon, since there the cost of living was low. . . .

Professor Heger

Charlotte and Emily, accompanied by Mr. Brontë, arrived at the Pensionnat Heger in Brussels on 15 February 1842, there

Charlotte Brontë, author of Jane Eyre, *was homeschooled by her father following the death of two of her sisters in boarding school.* Time Life Pictures/Time & Life Pictures/Getty Images.

to recommence the lives of schoolgirls at the ages of twenty-five and twenty-three respectively. The school's owner and directress was Claire Zoé Parent Heger, who was thirty-seven years old at the time of the Brontës' arrival in the rue d'Isabelle. In 1836 she had married Constantin Heger, a widower five years her junior, who taught at the Athénée Royal de Bruxelles; after their marriage, M. Heger retained his post at the Athénéé, but also assisted his wife in the operation of her school and gave classes there in literature. He was something of a romantic figure, having fought at the barricades during the Belgian revolution of 1830, and displaying a moody impetuousness that undoubtedly had a special appeal for one whose imaginary heroes had been similarly governed by violence of feeling. . . .

Heger's dominant personality, his acute intelligence, his position as mentor and friend, all combined to arouse in Brontë an admiration for one whom she could regard as her master. Had she been younger, her feelings might have taken the form of a schoolgirl infatuation, quickly roused and quickly quenched; but at twenty-six she had deeper yearnings, desires which possibly she did not understand herself. . . .

Her second year in Brussels began well; she was warmly received by the Hegers and promoted to the position of salaried teacher. She gave English lessons to M. Heger and his brother-in-law and continued her own studies in German; she paid frequent visits to her English acquaintances, the Dixons and the Wheelwrights. But without Emily's companionship . . . Charlotte felt increasingly isolated. Her relations with Mme Heger were deteriorating; to Emily she complained of Madame's aversion to her and expressed the belief that she was being spied upon. Allowing for an element of exaggeration in Brontë's complaints, there is little doubt that Mme Heger had become more guarded in her exchanges with the little English teacher; though Brontë never made any avowal of an attachment to Constantin Heger, her feelings must have been quite apparent to the shrewd directress of the pensionnat, who probably sought ways of reducing Brontë's opportunities for social contact with her husband....

At their parting, Heger had given Brontë a diploma attesting to her experience and qualifications; once back in Haworth, she hoped to make use of this in realizing the sisters' original plan of opening their own school.... Her efforts proved fruitless; not one prospective pupil applied, and by the close of the year the plan had been abandoned.

With the failure of the school project, Charlotte Brontë's life seemed to have reached a point of stagnation....

Charlotte and her sisters now entered a phase of literary production from which their brother was excluded.... In the autumn of 1845, Charlotte "accidentally lighted on a MS [manuscript] volume of verse" in Emily's handwriting and was immediately convinced that the poems merited publication. After Emily's initial reluctance had been overcome, the Brontë sisters set out to realize their long-cherished dream of authorship. *Poems by Currer, Ellis and Acton Bell* appeared in one volume at four shillings in May 1846; it received several friendly notices, but by June 1847 only two copies had been sold.

Writing Fiction

Lack of success in their first venture into print did not deter the sisters, however; even before the appearance of the *Poems*, they had already decided to try their hand at publishable fiction. In this they were doubtless encouraged by the enormous popularity of novels with the Victorian public. Thanks to such developments as part publication, cheap one-volume reprints, and subscription circulating libraries, a successful writer might now command a huge audience. The Brontë sisters were certainly impelled by the honorable motive of seeking critical applause, but undoubtedly they also hoped to turn their love of writing to good account and make some money by their pens....

Reaction to *Jane Eyre*

Maintaining her pseudonym of Currer Bell, Brontë sent off the manuscript of *Jane Eyre* on 24 August, five days after completing the fair copy. The book was accepted at once; within a month Brontë was correcting proofs; and on 19 October 1847, *Jane Eyre: An Autobiography*, "edited by Currer Bell," was published in three volumes at thirty-one shillings, sixpence.

The book won immediate and widespread acclaim. The *Times* called it "a remarkable production," a tale that "stand[s] boldly out from the mass." The *Edinburgh Review* saw it as "a book of singular fascination," and *Fraser's Magazine* urged its readers to "lose not a day in sending for it." Within three months the novel went into a second edition, and a third appeared in April 1848: no small achievement for a three-volume novel by a wholly unknown author. One of its first readers was the novelist [William Makepeace] Thackeray, who had been sent a copy by William Smith Williams; "exceedingly moved & pleased" by the novel, Thackeray asked Williams to convey his thanks to the author. Touched by this response, Brontë dedicated the second edition to Thackeray and added a preface expressing her admiration for the author of *Vanity Fair*, "the first social regenerator of the day."

In this chorus of praise, there were some discordant notes. The *Christian Remembrancer* for April 1848 commented unfavorably on the "extravagant panegyric" of the preface to the second edition, denounced the novel's "moral Jacobinism," and expressed displeasure at the author's attacks on Christian practice. Even more condemnatory was the unsigned notice in the *Quarterly Review* for December 1848, written by Elizabeth Rigby (soon to become Lady Eastlake). Jane Eyre is here described as "the personification of an unregenerate and undisciplined spirit," exerting the moral strength of "a mere heathen mind which is a law unto itself." The novel is accused of being "pre-eminently an anti-Christian composition," guilty of "a murmuring against the comforts of the rich and against the privations of the poor, which, as far as each individual is concerned, is a murmuring against God's appointment." The prevailing tone, one of "ungodly discontent," allies the novel in the reviewer's opinion to the cast of mind and thought "which has overthrown authority and violated every code human and divine abroad, and fostered Chartism and rebellion at home. . . ."

The plot of *Jane Eyre* might well disturb those to whom the divisions of social rank were sacred, since it follows the progress of a poor orphan from a loveless and humiliating dependence to happiness and wealth as an heiress and the wife of her former employer. Jane is an outcast, a rebel who triumphs over the forces of social convention expressed through caste, religion, and sexual tradition. Victorian readers were disturbed by the novel's suggestion that women need not always be passive or submissive, and by its treatment of love, which, by contemporary standards, seemed coarse and offensive. The supremacy of romantic love is an ancient theme in literature, but in *Jane Eyre* it was presented with a frankness and intensity new to English fiction. . . .

In December 1847 W.S. Williams suggested that Brontë write a novel for serial publication. She rejected this proposal but revealed that she was already planning a new three-volume novel based on a reworking of the materials she had used in *The Professor*. She made several attempts to begin this new work; one such commencement survives in the undated and untitled manuscript fragment known as "John Henry" or "The Moores," which describes the relationship between an overbearing mill owner and his intelligent, sensitive younger brother. The characters and framework of this story are strongly reminiscent of *The Professor*, but other elements, such as the characters' names and the younger brother's disdain for superiority based on rank or wealth, point toward *Shirley*. That novel began to take shape early in 1848, and Brontë made such steady progress that the first volume and part of the second were completed before the end of September. Then came a series of tragedies which ended all joy in composition and might well have destroyed the creative impulse in one less strong than Charlotte Brontë.

First, on 24 September 1848, came the death of Branwell. Though he had been declining for a long time, his death still came as a heavy blow to his family. Charlotte, who had been the most angry and embittered at his degenerate conduct, was the one who felt his loss the most deeply, and for several weeks after the funeral she was prostrated by grief and illness. This was succeeded by an even severer shock: Emily fell prey to consumption, and after a brief but heroic struggle, she died on 19 December 1848. More anguish was to follow; even before Emily's death, Anne's health had begun to deteriorate, and now she too suffered a rapid decline. In May 1849 Charlotte and Ellen Nussey took her to Scarborough in the hope that fresh sea air might bring some improvement, but she died there on 28 May, three days after their arrival.

Now, at thirty-three, Charlotte was the sole survivor of the six Brontë children. Grief and solitude weighed heavily upon her, but she pressed on with *Shirley*, finding in work an anodyne for her suffering; as she told William Smith Williams after the novel's completion, "the occupation of writing it has been a boon to me. It took me out of dark and desolate reality into an unreal but happier region." . . .

Exchanging Authorship for Marriage

With her marriage to Arthur Bell Nicholls on 29 June 1854, Charlotte Brontë's literary activity came to an end. The couple honeymooned in Wales and Ireland, returning at the beginning of August to Haworth (Charlotte could not be prevailed upon to leave her ailing father for long). . . . For the first time since the deaths of Emily and Anne, Charlotte Brontë found life at the parsonage congenial and satisfying; her new role as a wife kept her active and occupied, and her husband . . . daily revealed qualities which won her respect and increased her attachment to him. But the pleasures of this domesticity were short-lived. In January 1855 she discovered she was pregnant; she soon began to suffer from extreme nausea and vomiting, a condition which her delicate constitution was unable to bear. Worn out by the struggle, she died on 31 March 1855. Once more the house fell silent. Mr. Brontë remained there until his own death in 1861; Nicholls watched over him in his last years, then returned to his native Ireland, where he remarried in 1864.

The Brontë Sisters at Cowan Bridge School

Elizabeth Gaskell

Elizabeth Gaskell, a highly regarded nineteenth-century writer, whose most famous novel was Mary Barton, *was a personal friend of Charlotte Brontë.*

The following excerpt from Gaskell's famous biography of Brontë is about the school established for the daughters of clergymen, which all four Brontë sisters attended. There is no doubt that Lowood School in Jane Eyre *is patterned after Cowan Bridge School. Through research, Gaskell was able to document the rotten condition of the food, the extreme cold, a teacher's bullying of Maria, and the inadequate care provided for the many victims of typhoid fever at the school.*

About a year after Mrs Brontë's death, an elder sister . . . came from Penzance to superintend her brother-in-law's household, and look after his children. . . . The children respected her, and had that sort of affection for her which is generated by esteem; but I do not think they ever freely loved her. . . .

Cowan Bridge School

I do not know whether Miss Branwell taught her nieces anything besides sewing, and the household arts in which Charlotte afterwards was such an adept. Their regular lessons were said to their father; and they were always in the habit of picking up an immense amount of miscellaneous information for themselves. But a year or so before this time, a school had been begun in the North of England for the daughters of clergymen. The place was Cowan Bridge, a small hamlet on the coach-road between Leeds and Kendal, and thus easy of access from Haworth. . . .

There is nothing at all remarkable in any of the . . . regulations, a copy of which was doubtless in Mr Brontë's hands when he formed the determination to send his daughters to Cowan Bridge School; and he accordingly took Maria and Elizabeth thither in July, 1824.

I now come to a part of my subject which I find great difficulty in treating, because the evidence relating to it on each side is so conflicting that it seems almost impossible to arrive at the truth. Miss Brontë more than once said to me, that she should not have written what she did of Lowood in 'Jane Eyre,' if she had thought the place would have been so immediately identified with Cowan Bridge although there was not a word in her account of the institution but what was true at the time when she knew it. . . .

The Quality of the Food

When we—though I am not sure if I myself spoke—asked her some question as to the occasion she alluded to, she replied with reserve and hesitation, evidently shying away from what she imagined might lead to too much conversation on one of her books. She spoke of the oat-cake at Cowan Bridge (the clap-bread of Westmorland) as being different to the leaven-raised oat-cake of Yorkshire, and of her childish distaste for it. Some one present made an allusion to a similar childish dislike in the true tale of 'The terrible knitters o' Dent' given in Southey's 'Common-place Book:' and she smiled faintly, but said that the mere difference in food was not all: that the food itself was spoilt by the dirty carelessness of the cook, so that she and her sisters disliked their meals exceedingly; and she named her relief and gladness when the doctor condemned the meat, and spoke of having seen him spit it out. These are all the details I ever heard from her. She so avoided particularizing, that I think [the school's headmaster] Mr. Carus Wilson's name never passed between us. . . .

The Head of Cowan Bridge

A clergyman, living near Kirby Lonsdale, the Reverend William Carus Wilson was the prime mover in the establishment of this school. He was an energetic man, sparing no labour for the accomplishment of his ends. He saw that it was an extremely difficult task for clergymen with limited incomes to provide for the education of their children; and he devised a scheme, by which a certain sum was raised annually by subscription, to complete the amount required to furnish a solid and sufficient English education, for which the parent's payment of 14l. [pounds sterling] a year would not have been sufficient. Indeed, that made by the parents was considered to be exclusively appropriated to the expenses of lodging and boarding, and the education provided for by the subscriptions. Twelve trustees were appointed; Mr Wilson being not only a trustee, but the treasurer and secretary; in fact, taking most of the business arrangements upon himself; a responsibility which appropriately fell to him, as he lived nearer the school than any one else who was interested in it. So his character for prudence and judgment was to a certain degree implicated in the success or failure of Cowan Bridge School; and the working of it was for many years the great object and interest of his life. But he was apparently unacquainted with the prime element in good administration—seeking out thoroughly competent persons to fill each department, and then making them responsible for, and judging them by, the result, without perpetual interference with the details. . . .

Danger in Nature

Cowan Bridge is a cluster of some six or seven cottages, gathered together at both ends of a bridge, over which the high road from Leeds to Kendal crosses a little stream, called the

A portrait of the Brontë sisters (Anne, Emily, and Charlotte) painted by their brother Patrick Branwell Brontë. © Fine Art/Corbis.

Leck.... By the side of the little, shallow, sparkling, vigorous Leck, run long pasture fields, of the fine short grass common in high land; for though Cowan Bridge is situated on a plain, it is a plain from which there is many a fall and long descent before you and the Leck reach the valley of the Lune. I can hardly understand how the school there came to be so unhealthy, the air all round about was so sweet and thyme-scented, when I visited it last summer. But at this day, every one knows that the site of a building intended for numbers should be chosen with far greater care than that of a private dwelling, from the tendency to illness, both infectious and otherwise, produced by the congregation of people in close proximity. . . .

Condition of the School

The present cottage was, at the time of which I write, occupied by the teachers' rooms, the dining-room and kitchens, and some smaller bed-rooms. On going into this building, I found one part, that nearest to the high road, converted into a poor kind of public-house [tavern], then to let, and having all the squalid appearance of a deserted place, which rendered it difficult to judge what it would look like when neatly kept up, the broken panes replaced in the windows, and the rough-cast [plaster] (now cracked and discoloured) made white and whole. The other end forms a cottage, with the low ceilings and stone floors of a hundred years ago; the windows do not open freely and widely; and the passage up-stairs, leading to the bed-rooms, is narrow and tortuous: altogether, smells would linger about the house, and damp cling to it. But sanitary matters were little understood thirty years ago; and it was a great thing to get a roomy building close to the high road, and not too far from the habitation of Mr Wilson, the originator of the educational scheme.

The Filth of the School

Mr Wilson felt, most probably, that the responsibility of the whole plan rested upon him. The payment made by the parents was barely enough for food and lodging; the subscriptions did not flow very freely into an untried scheme; and great economy was necessary in all the domestic arrangements. He determined to enforce this by frequent personal inspection; carried perhaps to an unnecessary extent, and leading occasionally to a meddling with little matters, which had sometimes the effect of producing irritation of feeling. Yet, although there was economy in providing for the household, there does not appear to have been any parsimony [stinginess]. The meat, flour, milk, &c., were contracted for, but were of very fair quality; and the dietary, which has been shown to me in manuscript, was neither bad nor unwholesome; nor, on the whole, was it wanting in variety. Oatmeal porridge for breakfast; a piece of oat-cake for those who required luncheon; baked and boiled beef, and mutton, potato-pie, and plain homely puddings of different kinds for dinner. At five o'clock, bread and milk for the younger ones; and one piece of bread (this was the only time at which the food was limited) for the elder pupils, who sat up till a later meal of the same description.

Mr Wilson himself ordered in the food, and was anxious that it should be of good quality. But the cook, who had much of his confidence, and against whom for a long time no one durst utter a complaint, was careless, dirty, and wasteful. To some children oatmeal porridge is distasteful, and consequently unwholesome, even when properly made; at Cowan Bridge School it was too often sent up, not merely burnt, but with offensive fragments of other substances discoverable in it. The beef, that should have been carefully salted before it was dressed, had often become tainted from neglect; and girls, who were schoolfellows with the Brontës, during the reign of the cook of whom I am speaking, tell me that the house seemed to be pervaded, morning, noon, and night, by the odour of rancid fat that steamed out of the oven in which much of their food was prepared. There was the same carelessness in making the puddings; one of those ordered was rice boiled in water, and eaten with a sauce of treacle and sugar; but it was often uneatable, because the water had been taken out of the rain-tub, and was strongly impregnated with the dust lodging on the roof, whence it had trickled down into the old wooden cask, which also added its own flavour to that of the original rain water. The milk, too, was often 'bingy,' to use a country expression for a kind of taint that is far worse than sourness, and suggests the idea that it is caused by want of cleanliness about the milk pans, rather than by the heat of the weather. On Saturdays, a kind of pie, or mixture of potatoes and meat, was served up, which was made of all the fragments accumulated during the week. Scraps of meat from a dirty and disorderly larder, could never be very appetizing; and, I believe, that this dinner was more loathed than any in the early days of Cowan Bridge School. One may fancy how repulsive such fare would be to children whose appetites were small, and who had been accustomed to food, far simpler perhaps, but prepared with a delicate cleanliness that made it both tempting and wholesome. At many a meal the little Brontës went without food, although craving with hunger. They were not strong when they came, having only just recovered from a complication of measles and whooping-cough: indeed, I suspect they had scarcely recovered; for there was some consultation on the part of the school authorities whether Maria and Elizabeth should be received or not, in July 1824. Mr Brontë came again, in the September of that year, bringing with him Charlotte and Emily to be admitted as pupils. . . .

The Killing Cold

There was another trial of health common to all the girls. The path from Cowan Bridge to Tunstall Church, where Mr Wilson preached and where they all attended on the Sunday, is more than two miles in length, and goes sweeping along the rise and fall of the unsheltered country, in a way to make it a fresh and exhilarating walk in summer, but a bitter cold one in winter, especially to children like the delicate little Brontës, whose thin blood flowed languidly in consequence of their feeble appetites rejecting the food prepared for them, and thus inducing a half starved condition. The church was not warmed, there being no means for this purpose. It stands in the midst of fields, and the damp mist must have gathered round the walls, and crept in at the windows. The girls took their cold dinner with them, and ate it between the services, in a chamber over the entrance, opening out of the former galleries. The arrangements for this day were peculiarly trying to delicate children, particularly to those who were spiritless and longing for home, as poor Maria Brontë must have been; for her ill health was increasing, and the old cough, the remains of the hooping-cough, lingered about her.

Teacher Bullying

She was far superior in mind to any of her play-fellows and companions, and was lonely amongst them from that very cause; and yet she had faults so annoying that she was in constant disgrace with her teachers, and an object of merciless dislike to one of them; who is depicted as 'Miss Scatcherd' in 'Jane Eyre,' and whose real name I will be merciful enough not to disclose. I need hardly say, that Helen Burns is as exact a transcript of Maria Brontë as Charlotte's wonderful power of reproducing character could give. Her heart, to the latest day on which we met, still beat with unavailing indignation at the worrying and the cruelty to which her gentle, patient, dying sister had been subjected by this woman. Not a word of that part of 'Jane Eyre' but is a literal repetition of scenes between the pupil and the teacher. Those who had been pupils at the same time knew who must have written the book from the force with which Helen Burns' sufferings are described. They had, before that, recognised the description of the sweet dignity and benevolence of Miss Temple as only a just tribute to the merits of one whom all that knew her appear to hold in honour; but when Miss Scatcherd was held up to opprobrium they also recognised in the writer of 'Jane Eyre' an unconsciously avenging sister of the sufferer. . . .

I only wonder that she [Charlotte] did not remonstrate against her father's decision to send her and Emily back to Cowan Bridge, after Maria's and Elizabeth's deaths. . . .

Typhoid Fever

Before Maria Brontë's death, that low fever broke out, in the spring of 1825, which is spoken of in 'Jane Eyre.' Mr Wilson was extremely alarmed at the first symptoms of this. He went to a kind motherly woman, who had had some connection with the school—as laundress, I believe—and asked her to come and tell him what was the matter with them. She made herself ready, and drove with him in his gig. When she entered the school-room, she saw from twelve to fifteen girls lying about; some resting their aching heads on the table, others on the ground; all heavy-eyed, flushed, indifferent, and weary, with pains in every limb. Some peculiar odour, she says, made her recognise that they were sickening for 'the fever;' and she told Mr Wilson so, and that she could not stay there for fear of conveying the infection to her own children; but he half commanded, and half intreated her to remain and nurse them; and finally mounted his gig and drove away, while she was still urging that she must return to her own house, and to her domestic duties, for which she had provided no substitute. However, when she was left in this unceremonious manner, she determined to make the best of it; and a most efficient nurse she proved: although, as she says, it was a dreary time. . . .

The Death of Charlotte's Sisters

In the spring of [1825], Maria became so rapidly worse that Mr Brontë was sent for. He had not previously been aware of her illness, and the condition in which he found her was a terrible shock to him. He took her home by the Leeds coach, the girls crowding out into the road to follow her with their eyes over the bridge, past the cottages, and then out of sight for ever. She died a very few days after her arrival at home. Perhaps the news of her death, falling suddenly into the life of which her patient existence had formed a part, only a little week or so before, made those who remained at Cowan Bridge look with more anxiety on Elizabeth's symptoms, which also turned out to be consumptive. She was sent home in charge of a confidential servant of the establishment; and she, too, died in the early summer of that year. Charlotte was thus suddenly called into the responsibilities of eldest sister in a motherless family. She remembered how anxiously her dear sister Maria had striven, in her grave earnest way, to be a tender helper and a counsellor to them all; and the duties that now fell upon her seemed almost like a legacy from the gentle little sufferer so lately dead.

Both Charlotte and Emily returned to school after the Midsummer holidays in this fatal year. But before the next winter it was thought desirable to advise their removal, as it was evident that the damp situation of the house at Cowan Bridge did not suit their health.

Social Issues
in Literature

CHAPTER 2

Jane Eyre and Woman's Search for Independence

Female Independence as a Central Theme in *Jane Eyre*

Inga-Stina Ewbank

Inga-Stina Ewbank (died in 2004) was a Leeds University professor with expertise in a wide range of literature: William Shakespeare, Henrik Ibsen, August Strindberg, and the Brontës.

Unlike her sisters, Charlotte Brontë was passionate about her career as an author and "the woman question." In all her novels, Jane Eyre in particular, she pursues the ideal of independence for the unmarried woman. Independence encompassed not only economics and status, but personal identity and self-esteem. Brontë's authorship itself is part of a feminist rebellion against gender injustice. The earlier chapters of Jane Eyre are consistent with her vow to ignore the usual feminine stance and to tell the truth, to be a stark realist in picturing the exploitation of girls. By the time she reaches Thornfield Hall, she can say, "I care for myself," and Rochester respects her for her habit of speaking for herself. She is able to resist him and the despotic St. John, who is the opposite of life. Having the heart and the financial means, she can say when she refused St. John, "My powers were in play, and in force."

Unlike either of her sisters, Charlotte Brontë regarded her writing as a career. Unlike Anne she saw herself as a novelist rather than a moralist; unlike Emily she had literary ambition and saw her own work in relation to the tradition of the novel, 'It is my wish to do my best in the career on which I have entered', she wrote two months after the appearance of *Jane Eyre*; and the same note—writing as a deliberately chosen and pursued occupation which gives meaning and justification

Inga-Stina Ewbank, *Their Proper Sphere*. Edward Arnold, 1966. Copyright © I.-S. Ewbank 1966. Reproduced by permission of the Literary Estate of the author.

to her life—is sounded throughout her correspondence, until she enters on that all-too-brief second career of marriage, with all the responsibilities of a Victorian clergyman's wife.

The Ideal of Independence

Involved in, indeed inseparable from, her emphasis on the importance of a career is her attitude to the 'woman question'. . . . Charlotte, unlike either of her sisters, not only felt strongly about but also pronounced herself on the position of woman in society. Her letters show that she was interested in the many books and articles on the subject which were appearing in the late [1840s]. They also show that her interest was not of a reformatory kind and that she did not envisage the possibility of a fundamental change. 'Certainly there are evils which our own efforts will best reach', she writes to Mrs. Gaskell,

> but as certainly there are other evils—deep-rooted in the foundations of the social system—which no efforts of ours can touch; of which we cannot complain; of which it is advisable not too often to think.

What she did think about, and what forms the keynote in many of her letters, is the ideal of independence for the unmarried woman. A week before posting off to the publishers the volume that was going to be *Poems, by Currer, Ellis and Acton Bell*, she writes to her old teacher, Miss Wooler (in whose school she had also had a spell as governess), that, to her mind,

> there is no more respectable character on this earth than an unmarried woman who makes her own way through life quietly persevering—without support of husband or brother;

and the same theme runs through many of her letters in subsequent years, the success her novels met with and the lionisation she experienced on her few timid visits to London making little or no change in her attitude to herself as someone 'making her own way through life quietly persevering'.

Independence, then, is a keynote in her thinking about her own life and the life of all unmarried women. It is also a central theme in all her novels. . . .

In *Jane Eyre*, independence is much more a matter of status in the widest sense: personal identity and self-esteem. Jane measures her governess-ship at Thornfield Hall not by the wages it brings her but by the fact that, as she says to Rochester,

> 'I have not been trampled on. I have not been petrified. I have not been buried with inferior minds, and excluded from every glimpse of communion with what is bright, and energetic, and high. I have talked, face to face, with what I reverence; with what I delight in,—with an original, a vigorous, an expanded mind.' . . .

Economic Independence

In the novels of Charlotte Brontë, then, *homo economicus* [the man of economics] has turned female, and from one point of view her works are female success stories showing that hard work and good morals bring their reward. (Even Jane Eyre is rewarded with a legacy.) But we have already seen that this is not all. There may be 'no more respectable character on this earth than an unmarried woman who makes her own way through life quietly persevering'. . . .

A Woman Defiantly Speaking Her Mind

[Brontë] boldly points out that self-expression is a higher mode of art than writing for a 'purpose' ('Better the highest part of what is in your own self than all the political and religious controversy in the world'); and her publishers are firmly told:

> Unless I have something of my own to say, and a way of my own to say it in, I have no business to publish.

Here the theme of proud independence crops up again, now as an artistic principle, shaping her novels:

> Unless I can look beyond the greatest Masters, and study Nature herself, I have no right to paint. Unless I can have the courage to use the language of Truth in preference to the jargon of Conventionality, I ought to be silent.

Independence here means self-expression, in terms both of content and form, rather than art which is didactic and imitative. That she became aware of the difficulty of actually practising such imaginative autonomy within the framework of a novel and under the pressure of a reading public, we gather from the letter to Mrs. Gaskell, written several months after the publication of *Villette*, in which she speaks of the problem, when composing, of being 'quite *your own woman*, uninfluenced, unswayed by the consciousness of how your work may affect other minds; what blame, what sympathy it may call forth', and of how in such a situation a cloud seems to come between the writer and 'the severe Truth as you know it in your own secret and clear-seeing soul'. That the consciousness of how her work might affect other minds could be beneficial to her art we know from her own accounts of how *Jane Eyre* was written in response to publishers' criticisms of *The Professor*. That being true to the 'severe Truth' as she saw it, involved Charlotte Brontë in accusations of impropriety and coarseness, we also know. In this case her artistic principles brought her into conflict with the principles of conventional femininity and so involved her, willy-nilly, in a feminist rebellion. . . .

The Child Becomes a Woman

To Charlotte . . . realism in *Jane Eyre* lay above all in the Lowood chapters because, built on her experience at Cowan Bridge school, they faithfully reflected life as she had known it. To us the realism of the novel as a whole lies in its acute psychological observation, and the school section is realistic because it shows us, unmistakably, the mind of the child that was going to grow into Jane Eyre, the woman. They belong, structurally, in a novel which otherwise is largely about the Jane-Rochester relationship, because they are part of the logic that governs the book. That logic is one in which events appear only in so far as they affect Jane's mind: there is no sense of narrative material being brought in for its own sake; every incident and every character has a bearing on the growth of Jane into a woman of passion and absolute moral integrity. . . .

Jane's Control over Her Passion and Rochester

Jane is not only a girl with powers to attract a male; she is an *individual* whose key-line is: '*I* care for myself.' And so the later temptation scene becomes a microcosm of all human relationships, a vision of life.

But this is not to say that it reads, or is to be read, as an abstract allegory. I doubt if one could find in nineteenth-century literature a more concrete picture of desire reaching the point of no control than in Jane's description of Rochester as he threatens her with violence:

> His voice was hoarse; his look that of a man who is just about to burst an insufferable bond and plunge headlong into wild licence. I saw that in another moment, and with one impetus of frenzy more, I should be able to do nothing with him.

Or again later:

> . . . he crossed the floor and seized my arm, and grasped my waist. He seemed to devour me with his flaming glance: physically, I felt, at the moment, powerless as stubble exposed to the draught and glow of a furnace.

But this sentence continues: 'mentally, I still possessed my soul, and with it the certainty of ultimate safety'. She is safe, because her mind is impregnable, and because she knows her own value:

'*I* care for myself. The more solitary, the more friendless, the more unsustained I am, the more I will respect myself. I will keep the law given by God; sanctioned by man. I will hold to the principles received by me when I was sane, and not mad—as I am now.... They have a worth—so I have always believed; and if I cannot believe it now, it is because I am insane—quite insane: with my veins running fire, and my heart beating faster than I can count its throbs.'

And Rochester, too, recognises that without her soul and spirit she is not worth having. In the magnificent speech which begins 'Never ... never was anything at once so frail and so indomitable', he sees that spirit as a 'resolute, wild, free thing' looking out of her eyes; and then the bird-image, which we have noticed before, returns: her spirit becomes the bird and her body the cage,

'And it is you, spirit—with will and energy, and virtue and purity—that I want: not alone your brittle frame.' ... Rochester has come to love Jane *because of* her 'virtue and purity' and these are inextricably tied up with her 'will and energy'. Furthermore, it is because he recognises and allows that will and energy in her that Jane has come to love him; and because he recognises her as an individual who, though his social inferior, is spiritually not only equal but superior to him. It is significant that even at the crisis of, their struggle, Jane is able to enjoy her own sense of power:

I felt an inward power, a sense of influence, which supported me. This crisis was perilous; but not without its charm: such as the Indian, perhaps, feels when he slips over the rapid in his canoe.

Jane Refuses to Be Dependent on Rivers

We can see, then, that in the thematic structure of the novel, the St. John Rivers relationship is introduced as the antithesis to Jane's relations with Rochester. Physically, the two men are deliberately contrasted....

The physical contrast is a direct reflection of the spiritual one. When St. John asks Jane to marry him, she sees him thus:

> To me, he was in reality become no longer flesh, but marble; his eye was a cold, bright, blue gem; his tongue, a speaking instrument—nothing more.

His inhuman will is channelled into the one direction of self-sacrifice—anticipated in Charlotte's poem 'The Missionary'—and as he tries to force Jane's will in the same direction, their relationship develops into a step-by-step contrast with the Jane-Rochester story. Where Rochester recognised Jane's independent will, St. John, 'by degrees . . . acquired a certain influence over me that took away my liberty of mind'; and Jane speaks of her 'servitude' to him. Where Rochester stood for life and warmth and energy, St. John exercises over her a 'freezing spell' and becomes a sort of death-image: 'My iron shroud contracted round me,' says Jane, as his influence steals over her. His cold purity is the antithesis of life—

> if I were his wife, this good man, pure as the deep sunless source, could soon kill me: without drawing from my veins a single drop of blood, or receiving on his own crystal conscience the faintest stain of crime—

and his very proposal of a loveless marriage is death: 'If I were to marry you', says Jane to him, 'you would kill me. You are killing me now.' Partly because this situation is so far removed from the traditional romantic one, a modern reader may find it more uniquely perceptive than the Jane-Rochester relationship. Slowly St. John brain-washes Jane, using, in the final stages, his predestinarian religion to force her to believe that obeying him will mean election, while rejecting him would make her a 'castaway'. For the reading before family prayers on the evening in which their relationship reaches its climax, he chooses Chapter XXI in Revelation, the chapter about the new Jerusalem, 'prepared as a bride adorned for her husband'; and it is not the bride imagery but the antithesis between the blessed and the damned which is meant to work on Jane. . . .

Selfhood and Independence

As she breaks away from St. John, Jane sees her position as one of regained will-power, and thus regained identity:

> It was *my* time to assume ascendancy. *My* powers were in play, and in force.

And so, as a free individual as well as a passionate woman, she returns to Rochester.

In *Jane Eyre*, as we have already seen, the love story, the woman question and the governess (social) problem coalesce. Jane initially wins the love of Rochester through her own fearless sense of equality. . . . Her spirited assertion of equality is an essential step in the great love-scene in Chapter XXIII—'You glowed in the cool moonlight last night, when you mutinied against fate, and claimed your rank as my equal', Rochester says—and without it she would not have returned to ask Rochester to marry 'her who loves you best'.

Vision and Power in *Jane Eyre*

Peter J. Bellis

Peter J. Bellis, chair of the Arts and Humanities Department at the University of Alabama–Birmingham, is a widely published scholar and the author of Writing Revolution.

Early in their relationship, Rochester attempts to overwhelm Jane with his own strong vision, viewing her, as was customary at the time, as a dependent object because she was a woman. Her sex and rank get in the way of Jane's independent vision at Thornfield Hall, but Rochester comes to see that he cannot inflict his own vision on Jane, especially when he tries to force her to go away with him after she learns that he has another wife. It is only when Jane seeks out Rochester in the final chapters that both lovers are satisfied with a reversal in gender roles. As a blind man, Rochester has lost his dominant vision. Jane at the end must provide vision for him, is confident in her individual identity, and capable of writing her own narrative vision.

In *Jane Eyre*, sexual and social power is visual power. The struggle between Jane and Rochester is embodied in a conflict between two different modes of vision: a penetrating male gaze that fixes and defines the woman as its object, and a marginal female perception that would conceal or withhold itself from the male. The second alternative begins as a function of social and sexual dependence, but in the course of the novel Brontë redefines it as a position of both visual and narrative authority, the position from which the novel itself is written. . . .

Toward an Independent Vision

My argument here will be structured around three moments in the novel. The first, at Gateshead, establishes a pattern that the text will revise and ultimately reverse: Jane withdraws into a marginal spectatorship, only to be drawn out and exposed by an authoritative male gaze whose power is asserted through a culminating deprivation of vision. The second sequence, at Thornfield, alters the pattern; and the third, at Thornfield and Ferndean, inverts it altogether.

The novel opens with the ten-year-old Jane retreating from the Reed family group into another room. Taking a picture-book from the bookcase, she tells us,

> I mounted into the window-seat: gathering up my feet, I sat cross-legged like a Turk; and having drawn the red moreen curtain nearly close, I was shrined in double retirement.
>
> Folds of scarlet drapery shut in my view to the right hand; to the left hand were the clear panes of glass, protecting, but not separating me from the drear November day....

With the help of his sister Eliza, John Reed discovers Jane's hiding-place. Once she has been drawn out and exposed, he positions Jane before him and strikes her, "'for your sneaking way of getting behind curtains, and for the look you had in your eyes'"—in other words, for asserting her visual independence. John Reed claims the house and its contents as his, to be eventually inherited from his father's estate; for the additional crime of reading his book, he tells Jane to "'stand by the door, out of the way of the mirror and the windows.'" Cut off from both the outside world and even her own mirror image, Jane is forced to stand and watch John Reed aim the book at her head. The father's book is closed to her, he insists; she can only be the powerless victim of its oppressive force.

The son's vengeance is symbolically deepened when Jane's aunt sends her to the "red-room." The blinds are drawn down, the windows "shrouded" by red curtains—Jane is now enclosed in red on four sides, deprived of all external vision. Her only visual outlet is illusory, the merely apparent "depth" of a "great looking-glass," but she is nevertheless drawn towards its "visionary hollow". What she sees there is a "strange little fig-ure," an unrecognizable "phantom"—an alienated and specu-lar version of herself. She may not be the only "phantom" in the room, however: the "red-room" is where Jane's uncle, her surrogate father, had died; the mirror also "repeat[s] the va-cant majesty" of the paternal death chamber. As she dwells on the thought of her uncle's absence, "a light gleamed on the wall . . . while I gazed, it glided up to the ceiling and quivered over my head". This penetration by light is, for Jane, "a herald of some coming vision from another world"—a sign of the return of the dead father. She feels "oppressed, suffocated"; losing her self-control entirely, she screams and falls into "un-consciousness".

All these elements—retreat into a window-seat, exposure and interrogation, penetration by light, and a final loss of consciousness—reappear at Thornfield. But it is a repetition with a crucial difference, for it takes place in the context of an extended visual combat between Jane and Rochester, and it ends as an assertion of feminine, not masculine, power.

Independent Outside, Dependent Inside

Before Rochester's arrival, Jane often climbs to the roof of the house, where she can look "afar over sequestered field and hill and along dim sky-line". "I longed for a power of vision which might overpass that limit," she says, for she regards such visual power as the key to self-determination:

> safe in the silence and solitude of the spot [I could] allow my mind's eye to dwell on whatever bright visions rose be-fore it . . . best of all, [I could] open my inward ear to a tale that was never ended—a tale my imagination created, and narrated continuously; quickened with all of incident, life, fire, feeling, that I desired and had not in my actual existence. . . .

Inside the house, however, Jane is again in a position of social and visual dependence: even before their first formal meeting, Rochester tells her he has "'observed you—myself unseen,'" and he goes on to position her in the room as peremptorily as John Reed had done. . . .

Jane's Sex and Rank
Undermine Independence

The relationship between Jane and Rochester is dominated by visual exchanges, often followed by verbal exchanges about eyes and vision. . . .

"'I flatter myself,'" he says, that "'I read . . . your eye (beware, bye-the-bye, what you express with that organ, I am quick at interpreting its language). Then take my word for it,—I am not a villain.'" In turning looks into visible, *legible* words, Rochester is forcing Jane to "take *his* word," to accept her subordination to his verbal and visual power. It is a coercive desire of which Jane is very much aware: some time later, she remarks that "I wanted to hear his voice again, yet feared to meet his eye".

It is in this context of visual conflict that the pattern of events at Gateshead is repeated and transformed. When Jane and Adele are summoned to the drawing-room to join Rochester's house-party after dinner, Jane immediately "retire[s] to a window-seat" and takes up a book, exactly as at Gateshead. A crimson curtain hangs between the saloon and the drawing-room, separating her from the diners; when the curtain is swept back and the party enters, they settle into a static tableau, a visual spectacle with Jane as its unseen observer. She can describe them in detail only because she remains unnoticed; even when they realize that she is there, "behind the window-curtain", she remains socially invisible—as their snide comments on governesses demonstrate. . . .

If there remains a degree of visual and interpretive freedom in Jane's marginal, feminine position, it is one of which Rochester is well aware. Two nights later, he responds by at once parodying it and appropriating it to himself. He appears

Mr. Rochester lords over Jane in the 1944 film adaptation of Jane Eyre. Hulton Archive/ Stringer/Hulton Archive/Getty Images.

at Thornfield disguised as an old gypsy woman, wrapped in a red cloak. This assumed sexual and social marginality gives him the freedom to test the characters of all the women in the room; he summons them all, even and perhaps especially Jane, who "slip[s] out" last from her retirement, still "unobserved". . . .

Jane Returns with a Clear, Whole Vision

My primary emphasis here . . . is on the equally dramatic *literal* significance of Rochester's blindness: it gives Jane a tremendous visual power, one she both laments and exults in. When she arrives at Ferndean, she stands at the edge of its semi-circular garden and waits as Rochester emerges: "I stayed my step, almost my breath, and stood to watch him—to examine him, myself unseen, and alas! to him invisible". If Rochester's gypsy disguise had enabled him to enact a fantasy of sexual and visual power, his blindness gives Jane the same opportunity, a moment that she too is tempted to "protract *ad infinitum.*" If he once described her eye as birdlike, wild and free, she now compares him to a "caged eagle, whose gold-ringed eyes cruelty has extinguished."

She first watches him "grope his way" into the open only to turn and go back inside, and then follows him and taunts him. She brings him a glass of water, but will not identify herself, withholding her name until the last possible moment: "'Who is this? Who is this?' he demanded, trying, as it seemed, to *see* with those sightless eyes". It is only when he "gropes" for her—after she has forced him to rely on voice and touch—that she drops her game of blind man's buff and takes his hand, allowing him to guess her identity:

> "Is it Jane? *What* is it? This is her shape—this is her size—"
> "And this her voice," I added.

The next morning, Jane again enters the room 'very softly,' so that she may have 'a view of him before he discovered my presence', so that she may reassure herself of her new dominance. . . .

"I am still his right hand," Jane notes. By the time she writes her autobiography, Rochester may be able to read it, with her assistance, but he will never be able to write his own. When her visual power over him decreases, she asserts her textual power by writing, not the story of "Mrs. Rochester," but a book defiantly entitled *Jane Eyre*. If, on one level, Jane's goal is a union of voices, on another it is the assertion of individual, rather than marital, identity.

Parallels Between Colonialism and Female Oppression

Susan L. Meyer

Susan L. Meyer, a professor of English at Wellesley College, is the author of Imperialism at Home.

Jane Eyre, *written at the height of British colonialism, has multiple references to the oppressed people of India and Jamaica, countries that had been taken over by England. Brontë equates the subjugation of dark-skinned colonials with the domination of women and the lower-middle-class whites in England. Bertha, the madwoman in the attic, is symbolic of colonialism's victims. Her imprisonment in the attic is an example of colonialist tyranny. Jane refers to her own job as governess as being a slave, deprived of equality and independence. Jane also presents Bertha as a kind of double who can express Jane's own inner rage against the restraints of gender. After Jane's aborted wedding, slavery as Rochester's mistress looms over her. Bertha is the ultimate colonial revolutionary who cleans away social oppression with fire. Ironically, however, Jane gains her independence through English colonialism.*

Colonialism is ... present—and used figuratively—in each of Brontë's major novels. . . .

Brontë uses references to colonized races to represent various social situations in British society: female subordination in sexual relationships, female insurrection and rage against male domination, and the oppressive class position of the female without family ties and a middle-class income. She does so with a mixture of both sympathy for the oppressed and commonplace racism. . . .

Susan L. Meyer, *Victorian Studies*, vol. 33, Winter 1990. Copyright © 1990 Indiana University Press. Reproduced by permission.

In *Jane Eyre*, Brontë responds to the seemingly inevitable analogy in nineteenth-century British texts that compares white women with blacks in order to degrade both groups and assert the need for white male control. Brontë uses the analogy in *Jane Eyre* for her own purposes, to signify not shared inferiority but shared oppression. . . .

Imperialism at Home

While the perspective the novel finally takes toward imperialism is Eurocentric and conservative, I find in *Jane Eyre* not [critic Gayatri Chakravorty] Spivak's "unquestioned ideology" of imperialism, but an ideology of imperialism which is questioned—and then reaffirmed—in interesting and illuminating ways. . . .

Bertha and Other Imprisoned Women

Brontë's description of the room where Bertha has been locked up for ten years—without a window, with only one lamp hung from a symbolic chain—also reveals her awareness that the black-visaged Bertha . . . has ample reason to take revenge on a "violent race." In these moments in *Jane Eyre* Brontë subtly suggests that the history locked up in the English "shrine of memory" is one of "crime incarnate" in Bertha. But the "slavery" which Bertha's coloring and imprisonment suggest has a more deliberate figurative function. The numerous parallels that Brontë draws between Bertha and other characters in the novel suggest that her most important narrative function is to embody these parallels, to give them a vivid and concrete form.

The "slave" uprisings that Bertha's nocturnal violence evokes also have a figurative significance. As in her juvenilia [early works] and, less prominently, in her other major novels, Brontë uses slavery in *Jane Eyre* as a figure for economic oppression, a figure that the presence of Bertha illustrates and makes literal. . . .

Social Dependence and Dehumanization

As in her early African tales, Brontë does not use slavery as an analogy for the lot of the working class but for that of the lower-middle class, for those who are forced into "governess-ing slavery" as Rochester puts it. Jane's governessing at Thorn-field becomes like slavery to her only when Rochester arrives with his ruling-class friends and she experiences the dehumanizing regard of her class superiors. Before this, those around Jane treat her as a social equal. Mrs. Fairfax helps Jane remove her bonnet and shawl when she first arrives, and Adèle is too young and also of too dubious an origin to treat her governess with superiority. Brontë specifically constructs the atmosphere between the three of them—though significantly not between the three of them and the servants—as a utopian retreat from a world dominated by class hierarchy. Mrs. Fairfax distinctly marks the exclusion of the working class from this classless utopia when she tells Jane, just after expressing her delight that Jane has come to be her "companion": "you know in winter times one feels dreary quite alone, in the best quarters. I say alone—Leah is a nice girl to be sure, and John and his wife are very decent people; but then you see they are only servants, and one can't converse with them on terms of equality; one must keep them at a due distance for fear of los-ing one's authority". Some awareness of the costs even of hav-ing a class lower than one's own, a problem with which the novel is in general very little concerned, comes through in this passage. . . .

Slavery of Bertha and Jane

The imagery of social class slavery recurs in Jane's adulthood in the context of her awareness of the economic inequality be-tween her and Rochester. She comments after their engage-ment that receiving his valuable gifts makes her feel like a de-graded slave, and when he boasts that he will cover her head with a priceless veil, she protests that if he does she will feel "like an ape in a harlequin's jacket". Given the racist nineteenth-century association of blacks with apes, the apparition of Bertha's black face under the embroidered veil incarnates Jane's analogies.

This central passage, in which Jane glimpses Bertha's black face under the wedding veil, reflected in her own mirror, and then watches Bertha tear the veil in half, epitomizes the other form of slavery that Bertha both embodies for Jane and then enables her to avoid. Several feminist critics have commented on this passage, interpreting Bertha as either the surrogate or the double who expresses Jane's rage against the restraints of gender.

Jane Eyre associates dark-skinned peoples with oppression by drawing parallels between the black slaves, in particular, and those oppressed by the hierarchies of social class and gender in Britain. So far the narrative function of the dark-featured Bertha and of the novel's allusions to colonialism and slavery has a certain fidelity to history, although as the association between blacks and apes reveals (to take only one example), these analogies are not free from racism. In addition, this use of the slave as a metaphor focuses attention not so much on the oppression of blacks as on the situation of oppressed whites in Britain. Nonetheless, the analogies at least implicitly acknowledge the oppressive situation of the non-white races subjected to the British empire. . . .

During the period of Rochester's and Jane's betrothal, Brontë continues to use the imagery of slavery to represent Jane's lesser power in the relationship. But she veers away from making a direct parallel with the British enslavement of Africans by associating Rochester's dominating masculine power over Jane with that not of a British but of an Eastern slave master. This part of the novel is rich in images of Turkish and Persian despots, sultans who reward their favorite slaves with jewels, Indian wives forced to die in "suttee," [i.e., along with their dead husbands] and women enslaved in Eastern harems. The reality of British participation in slavery arises at one point in this part of the narrative—Rochester echoes the abolitionists' slogan when he tells Jane that she is too restrained with "a man and a brother"—but the novel persistently displaces the blame for slavery onto the "dark races" themselves, only alluding to slavery directly as a practice of dark-skinned people. At one point, for example, the novel uses strong and shocking imagery of slavery to describe the position of wives, but despite references to such aspects of British slavery as slave markets, fetters, and mutiny, the scenario invoked represents not British colonial domination but the despotic, oppressive customs of non-whites. Rochester has just compared himself to "the Grand Turk," declaring that he prefers his "one little English girl" to the Turk's "whole seraglio", to which Jane responds with spirit:

> "I'll not stand you an inch in the stead of a seraglio. . . . If you have a fancy for anything in that line, away with you, sir, to the bazaars of Stamboul, without delay, and lay out in extensive slave-purchases some of that spare cash you seem so at a loss to spend satisfactorily here."

> "And what will you do, Jane, while I am bargaining for so many tons of flesh and such an assortment of black eyes?"

> "I'll be preparing myself to go out as a missionary to preach liberty to them that are enslaved—your harem inmates amongst the rest. . . . I'll stir up mutiny; and you, three-tailed bashaw as you are, sir, shall in a trice find yourself fettered amongst our hands: nor will I, for one, cut your bonds till you have signed a charter, the most liberal that despot ever yet conferred." . . .

Freedom Associated with Cleanliness

Jane associates oppression and freedom with healthy and unhealthy environments. After she has fled Thornfield and settled at Morton, she reprimands herself for repining: "Whether it is better," Jane asks, "to be a slave in a fool's paradise at Marseilles—fevered with delusive bliss one hour—suffocated with the bitterest tears of remorse and shame the next—or to be a village schoolmistress, free and honest, in a breezy mountain nook in the healthy heart of England?". Jane here imagines the gender and class slavery she would endure as Rochester's mistress as a feverish, suffocating, southern atmosphere.

The damp pestilential fog of Lowood School is one of the novel's most drastically unhealthy environments; the atmosphere at this orphan institution where Jane thinks of herself as "a slave or victim" is the direct result of class oppression. After so many students die of the typhus fever fostered by the unhealthy environment, "several wealthy and benevolent individuals in the county" transform it into a less oppressive institution by the act of cleaning: a new building is erected in a healthier location, and "brackish fetid water" is no longer used in preparation of the children's food.

Creating a clean, healthy, middle-class environment stands as the novel's symbolic alternative to an involvement in oppression. . . .

Cleaning Is Like Revolution-Making

The other great cleaning activity in the novel occurs as Jane decides to "clean down" Moor House, and it marks a more successful attempt at washing away oppression than the one at Thornfield. Jane cleans the house to celebrate the egalitarian distribution of her newly acquired legacy, which will enable her to live there happily with her new-found family. Brontë writes of Jane's "equal" division of her fortune, using the rhetoric of a revolution against class oppression, although symbolically it represents a redistribution of wealth in favor of only a limited group of people, the lower-middle class. When St. John Rivers tells Jane that he, Diana, and Mary will be her brother and sisters without this sacrifice of her "just rights," she responds, in a tone of passionate conviction Brontë obviously endorses: "'Brother? Yes; at the distance of a thousand leagues! Sisters? Yes; slaving amongst strangers! I wealthy—gorged with gold I never earned and do not merit! You, penniless! Famous equality and fraternization! Close union! Intimate attachment!'". This sort of redistribution of wealth, Brontë suggests, giving Jane the language of the French revolution—*"Liberté! Egalité! Fraternité!"*—will right the wrongs of the lower-middle class, and clean from it the mark of blackness which represents oppression. Its women will no longer have to "slave" among strangers like blacks; its men will no longer have to venture into the distant, dangerous environment of the "dark races" in the colonies. With Jane, Brontë redefines the claims of "brotherhood," as her plot redistributes wealth: truly acknowledged "fraternity," the novel suggests, requires distributing wealth equally, not letting a brother or sister remain a penniless "slave." . . .

To signify her utopian end to economic injustice, Jane creates a clean, healthy environment, free of plague: her aim, she tells St. John, is "to *clean down* (do you comprehend the full force of the expression?) to *clean down* Moor House from chamber to cellar". Jane works literally to "set her own house in order," creating a clean, healthy, egalitarian, middle-class, domestic environment as the alternative to oppression. This environment is not, however, to the taste of St. John, who wants to force Jane into an inegalitarian marriage and to take her to the unhealthy atmosphere of British India (both of which she says would kill her), to help him preach his rather different values of hierarchy and domination to dark-skinned people. Jane recognizes this difference in mentality and their incompatibility when St. John fails to appreciate her housecleaning: "this parlour is not his sphere," she realizes, "the Himalayan ridge, or Caffre bush, even the plague-cursed Guinea Coast swamp, would suit him better".

Instead of deciding that it is her vocation to enter this new environment of plague, "dark races," and hierarchical oppression, Jane feels "called" to return to a house which, being larger and more stained by oppression, will be more difficult to "clean down"—Rochester's Thornfield. But of course when she gets there she finds that this "plague-house" has already been "cleaned down." Brontës plot participates in the same activity as Jane—cleaning, purifying, trying to create a world free of oppression. And the plot works precisely in the terms of the rhetoric of Jane's "revolution." It redistributes wealth and equalizes gender power, and it does so by cleaning away Bertha, the staining dark woman who has represented oppression.

In the ending of the novel, Brontë creates the world she can imagine free of the forms of oppression the novel most passionately protests against: gender oppression and the economic oppression of the lower-middle class. In the novel's utopian closure lies much of the revolutionary energy that made its contemporary readers anxious: the novel enacts Brontë's conception of a gender and middle-class revolution. The mutilation of Rochester (which interestingly has made critics of the novel far more uneasy than the killing of Bertha) and the loss of his property in Thornfield redistributes power between him and the newly-propertied Jane. Jane tells her former "master" emphatically that she is now both independent and rich: "I am," she says, "my own mistress". And in the last chapter Jane explicitly describes their marriage as egalitarian, unlike most: "I hold myself supremely blest beyond what language can express; because I am my husband's life as fully as he is mine". The closure of the novel also severely punishes Rochester for his acquisition of colonial wealth. . . .

Ironically, Colonialism Brings Jane Freedom

The atmosphere of Ferndean recalls the fact that, even if Rochester's tainted colonial wealth has been burned away, the wealth Jane is able to bring him, enabling her to meet him on equal terms—and the wealth she earlier distributes in such a scrupulously egalitarian and "revolutionary" spirit—has a colonial source. It comes from her uncle in Madeira, who is an agent for a Jamaican wine manufacturer, Bertha's brother. And the location of Jane's uncle John in Madeira, off Morocco, on the East Africa coast, where Richard Mason stops on his way home from England, also evokes, through Mason's itinerary, the triangular route of the British slave traders, and suggests that John Eyre's wealth is implicated in the slave trade. The details of the scene in which Brontë has Jane acquire her fortune mark Jane's economic and literary complicity in colonialism as well. St. John announces Jane's accession to fortune by pulling the letter out of a "morocco pocket-book", and he is able to identify Jane as the heiress because she has written her name, on a white sheet of paper, in "Indian ink".

In this way the novel connects the act of writing with colonialism. Specifically writing "Jane Eyre," creating one's own triumphant identity as a woman no longer oppressed by class or gender—or writing *Jane Eyre*, the fiction of a redistribution of wealth and power between men and women—depends on a colonial "ink." Whether advertently or not, Brontë acknowledges that dependence in the conclusion of *Jane Eyre*. Like colonial exploitation itself, bringing home the spoils of other countries to become commodities, such as Indian ink, the use of the racial "other" as a metaphor for class and gender struggles in England commodities colonial subjects as they exist in historical actuality and transforms them into East or West "Indian ink," ink with which to write a novel about ending oppression in England.

The Harem Slave and Rochester and Jane

Joyce Zonana

A professor of English at City University of New York, Joyce Zonana has published widely in journals. She is also the author of Dream Homes, *a memoir.*

Although Jane Eyre *gains her independence at the end, Zonana explains in this essay that* Jane Eyre *is filled with threats of enslavement, particularly with sexual overtones of the East. Every household she lives in, up to Ferndean, resembles a harem with a despotic male: John Reed, Brockhurst, Rochester, and St. John, all with several females under their control. Despotic Christian men are compared to extreme Muslims.*

> I proposed to myself to display the folly of those who use authority to bring a woman to reason; and I chose for an example a sultan and his slave, as being two extremes of power and dependence.
>
> *[Jean François Marmontel]*

On the day following Jane Eyre's betrothal to her "master" Rochester, Jane finds herself "obliged" to go with him to a silk warehouse at Millcote, where she is "ordered to choose half a dozen dresses." Although she makes it clear that she "hated the business," Jane cannot free herself from it. All she can manage, "by dint of entreaties expressed in energetic whispers," is a reduction in the number of dresses, though "these ... [Rochester] vowed he would select himself." Anxiously, Jane protests and "with infinite difficulty" secures Rochester's grudging acceptance of her choice: a "sober black satin and pearl-gray silk." The ordeal is not over; after the silk warehouse, Rochester takes Jane to a jeweller's, where "the more he bought me," she reports, "the more my cheek burned with a sense of annoyance and degradation".

Rochester as Sultan

The shopping trip to Millcote gently figures Rochester as a domestic despot: he commands and Jane is "obliged" to obey, though she feels degraded by that obedience. At this point in the narrative, Jane is not yet aware that in planning to marry her Rochester is consciously choosing to become a bigamist. Yet the image she uses to portray her experience of his mastery as he tries to dress her "like a doll" signals that not only despotism but bigamy and the oriental trade in women are on Jane's mind. Riding with Rochester back to Thornfield, she notes: "He smiled; and I thought his smile was such as a sultan might, in a blissful and fond moment, bestow on a slave his gold and gems had enriched." The image is startling in its extremity: surely Jane seems to overreact to Rochester's desire to see his bride beautifully dressed.

Yet by calling Rochester a "sultan" and herself a "slave," Jane provides herself and the reader with a culturally acceptable simile by which to understand and combat the patriarchal "despotism" central to Rochester's character. . . .

Brontë's use of feminist orientalism is both embedded in and brings into focus a long tradition of Western feminist writing. Beginning early in the eighteenth century, when European travelers' tales about visits to the Middle East became a popular genre, images of despotic sultans and desperate slave girls became a central part of an emerging liberal feminist discourse about the condition of women not in the East but in the West. . . .

Rochester's Repugnant References to a Harem

The feminist orientalism of *Jane Eyre*, furthermore, is only made explicit in the sultan/slave simile, and, although the chords struck in this passage resonate throughout the entire novel, they cannot properly be heard without an understanding of the full eighteenth- and nineteenth-century background that generates them. Before turning to that background, however, it may be helpful briefly to set in relief this key episode in which Jane not only compares Rochester to a sultan but engages with him in an extended discussion of women's rights and uses her comparison of him to a sultan as a means by which to secure more rights for herself.

Among the more interesting features of this passage is the fact that Jane does not tell Rochester that she is mentally comparing him to a sultan. She simply asks him to stop looking at her "in that way." Rochester is astute enough to understand Jane's unspoken reference, suggesting that feminist orientalist discourse is so pervasive as to be accessible to the very men it seeks to change: "'Oh, it is rich to see and hear her!' he exclaimed. 'Is she original? Is she piquant? I would not exchange this one little English girl for the Grand Turk's whole seraglio [harem]—gazelle-eyes, houri forms, and all!'". Rochester suggests that he will take Jane instead of a harem, though Jane bristles at the "Eastern allusion": "'I'll not stand you an inch in the stead of a seraglio' I said; 'so don't consider me an equivalent for one. If you have a fancy for anything in that line, away with you, sir, to the bazaars of Stamboul, without delay, and lay out in extensive slave-purchases some of that spare cash you seem at a loss to spend satisfactorily here'".

When Rochester jokingly asks what Jane will do while he is "bargaining for so many tons of flesh and such an assortment of black eyes," Jane is ready with a playful but serious response: "I'll be preparing myself to go out as a missionary to preach liberty to them that are enslaved—your harem inmates among the rest. I'll get admitted there, and I'll stir up mutiny; and you, three-tailed bashaw as you are, sir, shall in a trice find yourself fettered amongst our hands: nor will I, for one, consent to cut your bonds till you have signed a charter, the most liberal that despot ever yet conferred!" Although Jane promises Rochester that she will "go out as a missionary" to "Stamboul," the focus of her remarks is the reform of Rochester himself within England. Her concern is that she herself not be treated as a "harem inmate," and her action, immediately following this conversation, succeeds in accomplishing her goal.

Women's Slavelike Dependency

It is precisely Jane's experience of degrading dependency, playfully figured here as the relation of rebellious harem slave to despotic Eastern sultan, that leads her to take the step that ultimately reveals Rochester as more like a sultan than Jane had imagined. For it is at this point that Jane makes and executes the decision to write to her Uncle John in Madeira, in the hope that he will settle some money on her. "If I had ever so small an independency," she reasons, "if I had but a prospect of one day bringing Mr. Rochester an accession of fortune, I could better endure to be kept by him now". Jane's letter to John Eyre alerts Rochester's brother-in-law, Richard Mason, to Rochester's plans to become a bigamist, and Jane is freed from a marriage that would, in her own terms, have thoroughly enslaved her.

Jane's comparison of Rochester to a sultan proves to be no exaggeration. The narrative makes plain that it is because she sees him in this way that she later is able to free herself from a degrading relationship with a man who has bought women, is willing to become a bigamist, and acts like a despot. The plot thus validates the figurative language, making of it much more than a figure. This Western man is "Eastern" in his ways, and for Jane to be happy, he must be thoroughly Westernized. To the extent that Brontë has Jane Eyre present hers as a model life—"Reader, I married him"—she suggests that her female readers would also be well advised to identify and eliminate any such Eastern elements in their own spouses and suitors. . . .

The image of a harem inmate demanding liberty had by 1847 become so ingrained in Western feminist discourse that Brontë need not have had any specific text in mind; her audience, whether familiar with *Blue Beard* and *The Sultan* or not, would have had a full stock of harem images by which to understand and applaud Jane's sultan/slave simile. . . .

[The] image of domestic immurement . . . obviously haunts *Jane Eyre* and shapes its very structure. Examining this narrative structure, one sees that each household in which Jane finds herself is constructed to resemble a harem; each of her oppressors is characterized as a Mahometan despot; and each of her rebellions or escapes bears the accents of Roxanna, the harem inmate [in eighteenth-century French writer Baron de Montesquieu's *Persian Letters*] declaring her existence as a free soul. At Gateshead, at Lowood, at Thornfield, and at Moor House, one discovers a series of communities of dependent women, all subject to the whim of a single master who rules in his absence as much as his presence and who subjects the imprisoned women to the searching power of his gaze. In each of these households, Jane finds her own power of movement and of vision limited; even when she is most in love with Rochester at Thornfield, she recognizes that he stands in her way, "as an eclipse intervenes between man and the broad sun". . . .

Brocklehurst as Sultan

It may be objected that the ascetic aspects of Lowood accord ill with the suggestion that it is figured as a harem. Certainly Lowood harbors neither the sensuality nor the overt sexuality associated with the harem. Yet its structure, with one man controlling an indefinite number of dependent women, mimics that of the seraglio. Further, Brocklehurst's wish to strip the girls of all adornment, of all possibilities of sensual gratification, has its parallel in the sultan's wish to keep the women of the harem restrained from any sexuality not under his con-

To demonstrate Mr. Rochester's dominance over Jane, he is likened to a sultan while Jane is compared to a slave. Hulton Archive/Stringer/Hulton Archive/Getty Images.

trol. That Brocklehurst is figured in plainly phallic terms only underscores his identification as a sultan whose perverse pleasure here consists in denying pleasure to the women he rules. For his wife and daughters, however—women over whom presumably he can exert even greater control—Brocklehurst allows a greater sensuality: these women are "splendidly attired in velvet, silk, and furs". . . .

Rochester as Tyrant and Emir

Jane reveals that she is the governess at Thornfield; Rochester offers no information about himself, except to say, when Jane fails in her effort to lead his horse to him: "I see . . . the mountain will never be brought to Mahomet, so all you can do is to aid Mahomet to go to the mountain". Though uttered in jest, these words do not bode well for Jane's relationship with her master. Rochester gives himself the one name that, to a nineteenth-century audience, would unambiguously identify him as a polygamous, blasphemous despot—a sultan. After such an introduction, it comes as no surprise when Rochester chooses to dress "in shawls, with a turban on his head" for a game of charades, nor that Jane should see him as "the very model of an Eastern emir". . . .

Jane's Contradictions Regarding Religion

After Bertha's death, Rochester is free to reform, and this reform is significantly figured as a conversion: "Jane! you think me, I dare say, an irreligious dog: but my heart swells with gratitude to the beneficent God of this earth just now. . . . I did wrong. . . . Of late, Jane—only—only of late—I began to see and acknowledge the hand of God in my doom. I began to experience remorse, repentance, the wish for reconcilement with my Maker. I began sometimes to pray". The man who had passed a "Persian" law to justify his own behavior here acknowledges the authority of the Christian God who mandates monogamy and respect for the souls of women. Despite the many critiques of Christian ideology and practice that abound in *Jane Eyre*, Brontë's feminist orientalism here takes priority, as she obscures the patriarchal oppression that is also a part of Christianity.

And by ending her novel with the words of the Christian missionary St. John Rivers, himself one of the domestic despots Jane has had to defy, Brontë leaves the reader with an idealized vision of Christianity as the only satisfactory alternative to Eastern, "Mahometan"—and even Hindu—despotism. While this reversal in the characterization of St. John and the expressed attitude toward Christianity has struck many readers as a self-contradictory shift in Brontë's focus, it in fact confirms and seals the pattern begun with Jane's promise to "go out as a missionary to preach liberty to them that are enslaved".....

Jane's Brief Submission to a Despotic Religion

Though ... [the] identification of India as another Eastern site for the oppression of women is not in my view extensively developed throughout the text, it returns in the novel's conclusion, as well as in the penultimate section of the novel, when Jane faces the threat of being "grilled alive in Calcutta" if she chooses to accompany St. John to India. For during her stay at Moor House, Jane once again encounters a man with a "despotic nature" who rules over a household of dependent women and who threatens not only to immure but also to immolate her.

At first Jane finds Moor House less oppressive than her earlier homes. Yet when Jane consents to give up her study of German in order to help St. John learn Hindustani, she discovers another form of "servitude" and she experiences the kiss that St. John gives her as a "seal affixed to my fetters". Jane's subjection to St. John is in fact stronger than any she has felt before. "I could not resist him," she uncharacteristically admits. Part of Jane's difficulty in resisting St. John's wishes is that they come cloaked in Christian doctrine. Jane recognizes the despotism in St. John, knowing that to accede to his wishes would be "almost equivalent to committing suicide". Yet because St. John is a "sincere Christian", not an "irreligious dog," she has a harder time extricating herself from the seductions of his proposal that she marry him and accompany him to India: "Religion called—Angels beckoned—God commanded".

Brontë here reveals the motive behind feminist orientalism as a mode of cultural analysis as well as a rhetorical strategy. Jane finds it possible to resist Rochester because he calls himself and acts in ways that clearly echo the Western conception of "Mahomet," not Christ. But a man who assumes the language and posture of Christ is harder to combat. . . .

What St. John asks of Jane is that she abandon her already established love for Rochester. With this demand, he manifests what was, to Western feminists, perhaps the most threatening feature of "Mahometan" practice: interference with a woman's free choice of love object. . . .

Jane's Greatest Rebellion

In denying Jane her freedom to love (and in promising to impose the forms of sexual love upon her), St. John becomes the most brutal (and literal) of her harem masters and thus the one who evokes from her the greatest effort of rebellion.

Yet in the concluding paragraphs of the novel, St. John— the archetypal Christian man—is redeemed from the flaw in his own nature. By her resistance to his desire to enslave her, Jane frees him from his own oriental tendencies. If she is not a slave, he cannot be a master. Brontë makes explicit the implication behind [eighteenth-century English feminist author Mary] Wollstonecraft's assertion that the women of the harem have souls "just animated enough to give life to the body." A woman of soul, as Jane has by now firmly established herself to be, has the power not only to resist the harem but to transform it.

From Patriarchy to Matriarchy

Nancy Pell

Nancy Pell has written widely on women's issues and women authors, including Jane Austen, Charlotte Brontë, and George Eliot.

In the following essay Pell notes that beneath Jane Eyre, *the story of a girl's rebellion and individualism, one finds a critique of the middle-class male and his authoritarian religion. The domineering character of the patriarchy extends to the traditional religion which is used as a cruel tool by Brocklehurst and St. John. Jane's anticlericalism, developed in her search for independence, leads her to replace the old religion with a new matriarchal one, encompassing "the universal Mother, Nature." The epitome of hard religion is the Reverend St. John Rivers who is cold hearted and without love. He tells Jane that she was made for labor, not love. Jane already has the independent heart to handle the inheritance that gives her economic independence. Now she can say no to Rivers and approach Rochester as an equal. Pell describes Jane's marriage as "interdependence," rather than solitary independence. Although Jane and Rochester remain isolated and uninvolved, the reader should remember Jane's feminist concern for all women that she expressed from the balcony of Thornfield Hall.*

In *Jane Eyre* Charlotte Brontë's romantic individualism and rebellion of feeling are controlled and structured by an underlying social and economic critique of bourgeois [middle-class] patriarchal authority. Although this does not describe the entire scope of the novel, which includes countercurrents and qualifications as well, the formal and dramatic elements

Nancy Pell, "Resistance, Rebellion, and Marriage: The Economics of Jane Eyre," *Nineteenth-Century Fiction*, vol. 31, March 1977. Copyright © 1977 by The Regents of the University of California. Reproduced by permission of the publisher.

of a social critique are manifest in Jane's resistance to the illegitimate power of John Reed, Mr. Brocklehurst, and St. John Rivers; allusions to actual historical incidents involving regicide and rebellion; and, finally, the dynamics of Rochester's two marriages—both his marriage to Jane and his earlier marriage to Bertha Mason.

Jane's Early Resistance to Male Power

The dramatic presentation of Jane Eyre's struggles at Gateshead Hall involves the reader not only in the child's awareness of her oppression but also in the analysis of its source. . . .

The immediate origin of Jane's oppression is young John Reed, who spells out for her the basis for the contempt in which she is held. . . .

John Reed's position as sole male heir gives him an absolute power to harass his dependent female cousin. Jane is helpless against the silent complicity of the household; Mrs. Reed, Eliza, and Georgiana side with John, and Jane adds, "the servants did not like to offend their young master by taking my part against him". Not unknowingly Jane tells him, "You are like a murderer . . . a slave-driver . . . like the Roman emperors!" . . . Through the child Jane's interpretation of her suffering at Gateshead, Charlotte Brontë introduces the solid affairs "of the actual world" in terms of which the novel is to develop. . . .

Jane Fashions Her Own Religion

The Reverend Robert Brocklehurst, the "straight, narrow, sable-clad" minister, personifies the religious aspect of self-suppression and constraint that Jane will meet again in Helen Burns and St. John Rivers. Charlotte Brontë's picture of established spiritual authority in *Jane Eyre* is devastating. . . . Brontë goes beyond obvious anticlericalism to articulate an alternate religious system; she replaces the "mighty universal parent," the father God whom Helen Burns trusts and St. John presumes to represent, with "the universal mother, Nature", symbolized most often by the moon and its light. It is Nature's voice that urges Jane to flee temptation at Thornfield, as well as to return when she has come into her inheritance. Unlike "man," from whom in her wandering on the moors Jane anticipates only rejection and insult, Nature, whose guest and child she feels herself to be, "would lodge me without money and without price". The phrase is from Isaiah 55.1. Charlotte Brontë's use of biblical phrases and echoes, freely applied to Nature, Jane's mother, seems to me to point toward a matriarchal appropriation of traditionally patriarchal religious language. . . .

Staying Alive by Resisting St. John

Refusal to accept her death at the hands of others is Jane's chief motive for resisting St. John's commanding proposals of marriage. "You are formed for labour, not for love," he tells her, "I claim you—not for my pleasure, but for my Sovereign's service". His plan for Jane to conduct Indian schools feels to Jane like an iron shroud contracting around her, and his sister Diana imagines Jane "grilled alive in Calcutta". The argument about whether or not she will marry St. John is carried out in such images of death. It is a sacrificial death that Jane expects when she almost decides to accept his definition of her duty: "if I *do* make the sacrifice he urges, I will make it absolutely: I will throw all on the altar—heart, vitals, the entire victim". . . .

Jane's Relationship with Patriarchy

Rochester, as master, is unable to change, but Jane, as slave, is forced into change by the painfulness of the role she is forced to play. During their engagement, Jane continues to refer to him as her dear master; Rochester, however, loses sight of his "plain, Quakerish governess" and calls her his little elf, delicate and aerial, a sylph, an angel, a sprite or salamander. He insists on sending to London for heirloom jewels, which he will pour in her lap, and selects dresses for her of amethyst silk and pink satin. Jane finds his behavior peremptory, stubborn, and somewhat harassing. "The more he bought me, the more my cheek burned with a sense of annoyance and degradation. . . . He smiled; and I thought his smile was such as a sultan might . . . bestow on a slave his gold and gems had enriched". In this feverish atmosphere Jane becomes desperate to secure some independence from her future husband; she decides to continue as Adele's governess at thirty pounds a year and to write her uncle John Eyre to determine the prospects of any future inheritance.

The legacy that Jane receives from her uncle in Madeira makes possible her reunion with Rochester and also significantly redefines her relationship to patriarchal structures. "An independent woman now," Jane proceeds to redefine the term. Previously she has rejected the independence exemplified in Helen and St. John, who despise the natural and human realms of life. She has refused as well the mockery of independence found in Eliza Reed's advice to her sister Georgiana.

> "Take one day; share it into sections; to each section apportion its task: leave no stray unemployed quarters of an hour, ten minutes, five minutes—include all; do each piece of business in its turn with method, with rigid regularity. The day will close almost before you are aware it has begun; and you are indebted to no one for helping you to get rid of one vacant moment: you have had to seek no one's company, conversation, sympathy, forbearance; you have lived, in short, as an independent being ought to do."

Similarly, Jane turns down the role of heiress, which St. John urges upon her, and prefers a competency to a fortune.

Jane's legacy was built by her uncle on English trade with the West Indian colonies and on slavery, on the same base, in short, as Bertha Mason's attractive dowry. Jane accepts this inheritance, now invested in English funds, but she contradicts St. John's principled, capitalist argument in favor of her retaining the entire amount, which, she feels could never be hers "in justice, though it might in law". . . .

Jane's Independence and Equality

Their disagreement seems typical; St. John argues for that absolute possession of property that legal justice permits, Jane for the human justice of sharing with those she loves, whose needs she has experienced, by whose labors she has benefited. When the money first comes to Jane, in her isolation, she feels that "independence would be glorious"; but the "ponderous gift of gold" is transformed into a "legacy of life, hope, enjoyment" when she conceives the plan of dividing it with St. John, Diana, and Mary. Her experience of the accession of wealth becomes joy only when the personal reality of interdependence becomes economically possible.

"An independent woman now," Jane reappears at Thornfield. She has refused to be Rochester's mistress or St. John's mistress of Indian schools; now she is her own mistress and her proposal to Rochester is striking. "If you won't let me live with you, I can build a house of my own close up to your door. . . . I will be your neighbour, your nurse, your housekeeper. . . . I will be your companion. . . . you shall not be left desolate, so long as I live". Even their marriage can hardly be considered typically Victorian. Jane possesses a great deal of money in her own right, and although Rochester is far from the helpless wreck he is sometimes taken to be, he is dependent upon Jane "to be helped—to be led" until he regains his sight. He is troubled by what he calls his infirmities and deficiencies, but Jane, in lines that recall her recognition of equality with Mrs. Fairfax, declares "I love you better now, when I can really be useful to you, than I did in your state of proud independence, when you disdained every part but that of the giver and protector". Here, as earlier, equality must be real for Jane, not merely the result of condescension. . . .

Personal Not Social Change

Jane's affirmation of interdependence rather than of autonomy helps to explain the genuineness of her acceptance of Rochester, but it also points to the problem of their reabsorption into the system of inheritance and primogeniture that has made their earlier lives so difficult. Jane's division of her legacy among her cousins to secure each a competency is an important gesture . . . but the larger society remains unaltered. Both Rochester and Jane have acquired their wealth in untimely or arbitrary ways through the deaths of their predecessors in the line of inheritance. Together they have a son, who, in his turn, doubtless will inherit their combined estates.

Once they have found each other they withdraw from society altogether: "I am my husband's life as fully as he is mine," says Jane. "We talk, I believe, all day long". If they do not pander to house parties with neighbors like the Ingrams, neither do they travel beyond Rochester's property to "the busy world, towns, regions full of life . . . acquaintance with variety of character", for which Jane had longed at Thornfield. Ten years after their marriage Jane and Rochester are still sequestered at Ferndean Manor, always a place of dubious healthfulness and damp walls, seeing only the servants and, once a year, Diana and Mary Rivers and their husbands. . . .

Independence for All Women

Yet the struggle is not utterly isolated. In the central feminist assertion of the novel Jane looks out from the rooftop of Thornfield Hall and confesses to feeling discontented and restless. At this moment her strivings are more than simply the effort for individual survival; there is a sense of comradeship with other women of her class.

> Millions are condemned to a stiller doom than mine, and millions are in silent revolt against their lot. Nobody knows how many rebellions besides political rebellions ferment in the masses of life which people earth. Women are supposed

to be very calm generally: but women feel just as men feel; they need exercise for their faculties, and a field for their efforts as much as their brothers do; they suffer from too rigid a restraint, too absolute a stagnation, precisely as men would suffer. . . . It is thoughtless to condemn them, or laugh at them, if they seek to do more or learn more than custom has pronounced necessary for their sex.

Balancing Romance
and Independence

Jean Wyatt

Jean Wyatt, a professor of English at Occidental College in Los Angeles, studies and writes on the intersection of gender and race and psychoanalysis and is the author of Risking Difference: Identification, Race and Community in Contemporary Fiction and Feminism.

In this essay Wyatt raises the question of whether Jane Eyre *reinforces patriarchal patterns of female life or whether she resists them. The answer Wyatt gives is that the novel highlights many frustrations with gender inequalities in a patriarchal society. Rochester has the role of the supreme patriarch—the father; Jane has the role of the defiant daughter. The situation creates romance but also protest against authority. Perhaps the old romantic fantasies can be changed into liberating ones. Rochester's power and experience make him an alluring figure in the old romantic tradition. Wyatt argues that Jane and her readers are able to channel this fantasy into liberating energy. Until she achieves independence, Jane's individualism is continually thwarted. Even Rochester tries to impose his patriarchal view of woman on the resisting Jane. When she returns to Rochester, the patriarchal romance has turned into a marriage of equality— each partner bound by love but retaining a separate self. Still, beneath Jane's treasured independence runs a river of romantic passion for her very own patriarch.*

I want to explore the interaction between novels and female fantasy patterns by asking two related questions about reader response to *Jane Eyre*. First, how can we explain that

Jean Wyatt, "A Patriarch of One's Own: Jane Eyre and Romantic Love," *Tulsa Studies in Women's Literature*, vol. 4, Autumn 1985. Copyright © 1985, The University of Tulsa. Reproduced by permission of the publisher and the author.

women widely separate in time and nationality share psychic patterns that make them recognize in *Jane Eyre* hidden truths about their own inner lives? Second, since girls often read *Jane Eyre* at a formative time in their lives, what fantasies does it offer them? Does it reinforce fantasy patterns acquired from growing up female in the Western nuclear family, or does its appeal come from the pattern of resistance to patriarchal forms? . . .

Resistance to Patriarchy

In fact, *Jane Eyre* is rich in fantasies addressed to the frustrations of growing up female in a white middle-class family structure skewed by the unequal distribution of power and mobility along gender lines: fantasies of a young girl's defiant autonomy, fantasies of a good mother (Miss Temple) and a bad mother (Mrs. Reed), and fantasies of revenge on bullying brothers and prettier sisters (the Reed children). Perhaps most appealing, at least to a female reader with a strong, dominant father who fits the patriarchal model, Rochester offers Jane the excitement combined with frustration and enigma that characterize father-daughter interactions. By showing how the extraordinarily complicated sexual politics between Jane Eyre and Rochester reflect the convolutions of father-daughter relations in a nuclear family where the mother is largely responsible for childcare, the father for work outside the home, I hope to make the broader point that some structural features of romantic love are grounded in traditional patterns of relationship between fathers and daughters. Against the pull of its patriarchal love fantasy, *Jane Eyre* presents an equally passionate protest against patriarchal authority. The contradiction, I claim, mirrors a female reader's ambivalence toward her father. Part of *Jane Eyre*'s appeal lies in the way it allows girls (and women) to work out fantasies of desire and rage against fathers that stem from the power and inaccessibility of a father in a traditional Western family structure and his ambiguous position in regard to his daughter's sexuality.

Jane Eyre exerts a powerful attraction on female readers partly because it combines unconscious fantasies centering on Bertha Mason—fantasies that appeal directly to the unconscious quirks of a woman brought up in this culture—with political analysis directed by Jane at the reader's conscious mind. While Jane reasons out the causes and effects of women's domestic oppression, Bertha burns down the imprisoning house. This combination of revenge fantasy with conscious political analysis raises the question: can a novel release the energy stored in a reader's unconscious fantasies of rage against patriarchal family structures and rechannel it into a desire for social change? . . .

Perhaps novels that involve readers on the passionate level of their own most cherished fantasies do not merely allow them to revel in infantile fantasies, but afford them the extra pleasure of releasing the energy buried in old restrictive fantasy patterns and rechanneling it into new, potentially liberating ones. . . .

Rochester as Patriarch

Rochester slips right into the slot prepared for him in the reader's unconscious: "I am old enough to be your father," he reminds Jane at intervals. "I have . . . roamed over half the globe, while you have lived quietly with one set of people in one house". Mastery of the wide world, freedom, autonomy are his. Jane remains enclosed in *his* home, subordinate to him and subject to his orders, in a position parallel to a girl's in her father's household. Far above Jane in rank and power, Rochester seems inaccessible; his mysterious absences and even more mysterious broodings over his hidden inner life endow him with the glamor of the unknown and make him a target for idealization. . . .

Female Containment

Brontë's insistent imagery of female containment must appeal to female readers' angry memories of bumping up against the walls of parental sex role definitions. And Jane's repeated, and repeatedly thwarted, attempts to gain autonomy must call up the anger associated with her female readers' similarly frustrated declarations of independence. Whenever Jane claims the right to her own identity, the patriarchy inevitably puts her in her place: being locked into the Reeds' Red Room is only the most forcible of her confinements to the gender compartments of the patriarchal family. Jane's angry response to all attempts to define her as a subordinate is one of defiant autonomy: "I am not an angel . . . I will be myself". Jane's repeated refusals to be contained within gender categories can inspire her reader with a similar determination to make the fantasy of autonomy a reality in her own life.

If Jane's verbal defiance of patriarchal restrictions presents the reader with an appealingly noble image of herself as brave resistance fighter, Bertha satisfies the reader's anger against patriarchal constraints on a more primitive level. Bertha raging in triumph on the battlements of the burning house, Rochester pinned beneath by its falling pillars, must gratify a female reader's repressed rage against her father and the whole patriarchal family structure that limits female aspiration.

This combination of Jane's verbal protest with Bertha's vivid action is only one example of the way Brontë uses Bertha and Jane to lodge a powerful protest against women's oppression at all levels of her reader's psyche. Bertha, appropriately preverbal (she groans, screams, mutters, and laughs, but never speaks) addresses the quirks of a female unconscious through images of painful incarceration and fiery revenge. Jane appeals to the reader's intellect with a social analysis of how confinement in domestic structures damages women. While Bertha demonstrates, Jane articulates the causes of her madness. Brontë thus manages to appeal to the reader's unconscious fantasies of revenge while analyzing the social oppressions that cause them.

Jane retains her independence through the course of the novel and marries Mr. Rochester, which eventually leads to the idea that they have an equal partnership. © Bettmann/ Corbis.

A fairly simple example of their collaboration occurs when Jane makes her famous third-story speech against the confinement of women to domestic tasks; as she finishes elaborating the damages that can result from "too rigid a constraint, too absolute a stagnation," Bertha's mad laughter rings out in confirmation. . . .

Male Definition of Women

Part of the constriction Jane (and, one supposes, Bertha) feels comes from the readiness of patriarchal authority both to define female propriety and to punish infractions of it. Just as Rochester banned Bertha for being "intemperate and unchaste," St. John unhesitatingly brands Jane's words "violent and unfeminine", punishing her with a spiritual isolation that is the counterpart of Bertha's solitary confinement. But allowing St. John to impose his definition of female virtue on her— "you are docile, diligent, disinterested, faithful, constant and courageous; very gentle, and very heroic"—makes Jane feel threatened, too. Her desires, vague and diffuse before, "assumed a definite form under his shaping hand . . . my iron shroud contracted around me". The metaphor extends the constraint of Bertha's prison cell to an image of deadly spiritual constriction. Jane's repetition of death images implies that both succumbing to patriarchal definitions and braving them imperil her survival as an individual. . . .

Love and Equality

In the next to last chapter, Jane returns to Rochester a new woman—that is, rich and independent. Since Bertha has burned down Thornfield, Jane and Rochester are free to build a new domestic structure from the ground up. At first they seem emotionally free, too, to imagine new ways of living together. In a bantering review of alternative structures, Rochester suggests—yet again!—that they could be father and daughter to each other, or nurse and patient. Jane boasts of her new independence: "I can build a house of my own close up to your door". As an alternative to the hierarchy of a patriarchal household, the model of houses side by side embodies a notion of marriage as "parallel lives," in [literary critic] Phyllis Rose's phrase: together, yet with a margin of separation, husband and wife would be equally powerful and autonomous, equally masters of their own houses.

This vision of a separate and equal love is but the creation of a moment's imaginative freedom, though, swept away almost immediately by the ideology of love that floods the last chapter. It begins with a cry of triumph: "Reader, I married him!" Brontë forgets her own powerful argument against the constraints of being a *wife* to embrace the happy ending of romantic fantasy. . . .

But I suspect that many modern readers, including feminists like myself, are attached to *Jane Eyre* because it reflects so well our ambivalence. On the level of lucid and compelling rhetoric, Brontë advocates feminist ideals—arguing against patriarchal structures that confine and subordinate women and for a wider field for women's endeavors—while underneath flows, unchecked, a passionate desire for the fusions of romantic love. Those of us who, like Brontë, grew up in patriarchal family structures with an attachment like hers to a strong father probably share with her a susceptibility to the ideology of love at odds with ideological conviction. I suspect that the way conscious autonomous and egalitarian structures operate as covers for unconscious desire throughout the last two chapters mirrors our genuine efforts to structure our lives differently, only to be sabotaged by our own unregenerate desires for fusion with a patriarchal figure. Jane founds a broad base for autonomy at Moor House, but abandons it for Rochester's narrow embrace: evidently a community that offers only respect and self-respect based on productive work and financial independence, along with family warmth and female solidarity grounded in shared intellectual pursuits and emotional kinship, isn't enough; passionate love is. The careful restructuring of power that seems to promise something new—an egalitarian basis for marriage with a bit of leeway for wifely autonomy—gives way to the rhapsody on marital fusion. The superficial political fantasy of redistributed power covers underlying images of symbiosis with a strong oak of a man. I suspect that just as erecting a new structure for marriage enables Brontë to dream an old dream, so the apparently revolutionary nature of Jane's egalitarian marriage allows an old fantasy to get by the ideological censors of her readers, so that we all, feminists and Harlequin romance readers alike, can enjoy the unending story of having one's patriarch all to oneself forever.

Romance Is Not Compatible with Freedom

Melodie Monahan

Melodie Monahan has a PhD in English and runs Inkwell Works, an editing service. The works of Charlotte Brontë are her specialty.

Jane Eyre's reading of her favorite book, Gulliver's Travels, *heightened her desire for the freedom allowed males to seek adventure, both literally and mentally. But when she enters the male sphere, she is drawn to the safety and connections of the domestic scene. The quest and romance seem contradictory, but the woman who feels the power of her revolt fights against dependency. Such a woman, as is Jane, when she resists male tyranny, will find herself marginalized within the household. But if she does not rebel and is taken into the family, she will still find herself dependent. Traditional romance is derailed in* Jane Eyre *as the plain heroine insists on her own adventure and fights against inequality. But independence is in conflict with romance, which devalues women. Still, by the end of the novel Jane is finally able to achieve equality and independence in the male romance.*

To comfort Jane Eyre after her trauma in the red room, Bessie brings Jane's favorite book, *Gulliver's Travels*. Considering her former responses to modes of fantasy, Jane explains how she now reads the text differently (emphasis added):

> This book I had again and again perused with delight; I considered it a *narrative of facts*, and discovered in it a vein

of interest deeper than what I found in fairy tales: for as to the elves ... I had at length made up my mind to the *sad truth* that they were all gone out of England ... whereas, Lilliput and Brobdingnag being, in my creed, solid parts of the earth's surface, *I doubted not that I might one day, by taking a long voyage, see with my own eyes* the little fields, houses, and trees, the diminutive people, the tiny cows, sheep, and birds of the one realm; and the corn-fields forest-high, the mighty mastiffs, the monster cats, the tower-like men and women, of the other. Yet, when this cherished volume was now placed in my hand—when I turned over its leaves, and sought in its marvelous pictures the charm I had, till now, never failed to find—all was eerie and dreary; the giants were gaunt goblins, the pygmies malevolent and fearful imps, Gulliver a most desolate wanderer in most dread and dangerous regions. I closed the book, which I dared no longer peruse.

Jane's Desire for the Quest

Jane's earlier response asserted the authority of *Gulliver* and its relevance to her own experience: if not in England, then at least somewhere and someday she believed she could replicate its quest model. But now, subjugated by the Reeds, Jane finds both the world of the text and her own reality darkened. In the same scene she notes how the painted plate is strangely faded: and how Bessie's once lively tune now resounds like a "funeral hymn".... Sudden self-awareness of her female status ... dispels for Jane the promise of escape ... and makes problematic her once easy identification with male questers.

Jane Cannot Have Both Adventure and Romance

All of a sudden, for Jane as female reader and hero, quest-romance breaks apart: instead of a hyphenated whole, a linear progression, the pattern confounds with a mixed message. From the female hero's point of view, quest-romance is self-contradictory. . . . On the one hand, quest beckons her, like her male counterparts, to head out in search of stimulus and adventure, to find another perhaps better world. But on the other hand, romance invites her into the patriarchal home where female autonomy is sacrificed for safety and connection. Clearly; the contradiction is gender-specific. Heading out *is* going home for the male hero in at least the one sense that he exists in an androcentric [male-centered] culture, and he has access to male privilege whether he is in the world or at home. The female's relationship to both heading out and going home are problematic, particularly so when the two are conjoined. The woman who undertakes the journey and feels the struggle and empowerment in her revolt against marginality will resist subordination in a household. . . .

The Female's Loss of Status in Romance

Heading out is the quest form seen in *Jane Eyre* in Jane's repeated departures from households, from Gateshead, Lowood, and Thornfield. Going home is enacted each time Jane establishes community, at Lowood with Miss Temple and Helen, at Thornfield with Rochester and Adele, and at Marsh-End with Diana and Mary Rivers. Heading out breaks down in the nadir of Whitcross and the night on the moors. Going home accrues with the establishment of the Morton Cottage school and the recognition of the Rivers as relatives; it culminates in the family found at last with Rochester and a son. The recurrent ambivalence, however, undermines any final claim of perfect happiness. Each cycle in this female enactment of quest-romance turns in against itself; what the female hero is as a questing protester against patriarchal tyranny, she cannot be as an assimilated member who connects and stabilizes with others. To end the search is to settle for the known; to become a member of the group is to forget the feel of alienation. For male and female heroes alike, to quest is to test the power within and have the chance of self-determinism. But for the female hero, to be absorbed, then, into the patriarchal economy of romance is to be relegated to the homebound periphery of action and into the margins of importance. . . .

Traditional Romance Derailed in *Jane Eyre*

Let us first consider how Brontë derails traditional romance and its heroine. The romantic legacy she displaces in *Jane Eyre* consists of programmatic scenarios which trap beautiful, middle- and upper-class heroines in passive, mimetic roles. . . . Automatically an insider the beautiful heroine symbolizes the prevailing ethic that physical appearance is the first measure of female worth. Moreover, the script she inhabits maximizes the erotic and leaves no psychic dimension or literal space for non-erotic female ambition, the quest.

Jane Resists Oppressive Conventions

Jane's journey is both a literal leave-taking from oppressive hierarchical groups and a process of negotiating for lateral connection. The quest for a better world expresses itself in her repeated efforts to challenge binary and vertical constructs: the haves and the have-nots, the saved and the damned, the insiders and the outcasts, the masculine and the feminine. A noteworthy early example of this insurgence is her tart reply to Brocklehurst's idea that hell consumes the wicked. To avoid hell fire, Jane asserts, "I must keep in good health, and not die". In response to Helen Burns's excessive compliance with Christ's Doctrine of Love, Jane powerfully contends that equality is worth fighting for: "If people were always kind and obedient to those who are cruel and unjust, the wicked people would have it all their own way: they would never feel afraid, and so they would never alter, but would grow worse and worse. When we are struck at without a reason, we should strike back again very hard; I am sure we should—so hard as to teach the person who struck us never to do it again". Jane repeatedly speaks and acts in an attempt to topple the sanctioned superstructures of social and literary design. . . .

Jane Dismisses Patriarchy

Repeatedly we see in *Jane Eyre* how the narrative exposes the prevailing group's cruelty in imposing arbitrary prerogatives on inferiors. In the Reeds' bullying at Gateshead, in the hypocrisy of Brocklehurst and his family at Lowood, in the sanctioned ostracism of the governess by the drawing-room guests at Thornfield, even in Hannah's attempt to reject the destitute Jane on the doorstep at Marsh-End, we see the group's mechanism of exclusion and self-aggrandizement. These communities share the hierarchical and superficial values of monied society; they endorse the arbitrary power of privileged birth and the middle- and upper-class objectification of women. When ten-year-old Jane wonders, "Why could I never please?" she cites her physical plainness as cause, for Georgiana's beauty seems "to purchase indemnity for every fault". The novel opens on the day when "the mad cat" chooses no longer to "endure the blow": on the day when, Jane Eyre admits, "I resisted all the way: a new thing for me". Conjuring tumult and insurrection, Jane becomes an "infantine Guy Fawkes". Midway through the novel, Aunt Reed remembers dealing with Jane Eyre on that first day: "I felt fear, as if an animal that I had struck or pushed had looked up at me with human eyes and cursed me in a man's voice". As Jane speaks the truth, she acquires rank: the "animal" in her seems human; its voice sounds male. By asserting her own facts Jane wins space as well as status: "my soul began to expand, to exult, with the strangest sense of freedom, of triumph". Empowered by protest, Jane subverts the system which attempts to devalue her. . . .

The Conflict Between Romance and Selfhood

With Jane's sexual maturation and the advent of Rochester, the contradictory imperatives of quest-romance become more explicit. Jane's need for a sexual partner, for kinship and a sense of home are at variance with her need to achieve autonomy through self-sufficiency and through the process both as teacher and author of defining reality from her own perspective. Coupled with these difficulties are the special problems of Rochester's past, his conditioning with regard to sex roles, and his perverse experience with marriage. . . . Though loving Rochester subjects Jane to the very system which devalues her, she continues to resist the assigned passivity of marginal status and becomes here the active negotiator, one who can set some conditions, one who can comply or refuse. In this give-and-take process, the quest impulse reroutes romance, creating a fantasy about equitable partnership that requires both female empowerment and male reduction. This emergent fantasy is constantly undermined, however. . . .

Jane Achieves Selfhood in a Male Romance

Against this traditional economy of male dominance in marriage, Jane's narrative envisions another structure for heterosexual love.

In this new structure, power is distributed so that the female role can be defined as essential not extraneous, useful not decorative. So that while romantic attachment seems to disempower Jane by drawing her like a "magnet" to Rochester, it also enhances her with vitality and gives her "keener hopes". In her evening conversations with Rochester, Jane recognizes her "power to amuse him", not as an entertainer like Blanche singing and playing the piano, but rather as one who can help him realize a sense of communion, a oneness that supersedes the hierarchy of class and the polarization of gender. Validated as an individual through her connection to Rochester, Jane can visit her dying aunt and discover that a sneer is "no longer powerful". She can see that for Aunt Reed the lament "we are getting poor" veils the terrifying realization of common mortality. Jane can *now forgive* the unforgiving. I would assert, moreover, that her attachment to Rochester, entailing as it does the enhancement of female power, prevents Jane's victimization in the narrative Rochester would himself authorize, one which evolves through sadistic teasing about Blanche to his hope for a bigamous marriage and his final desperate plea for an extramarital alliance, all painful distortions of the romance script.

Against Rochester's seemingly endless machinations and lies, Jane remains resistant and powerful. Though she claims she would give her life to serve him, Jane still negotiates the terms of her connectedness: "I am no bird; and no net ensnares me: I am a free human being with an independent will". Later she calls his proffered engagement gifts "a degradation." In courtship she shows Rochester "the rugged points" of her character, noting and resisting his desire to "attach [her] to a chain". In his description of former illicit relationships, she hears his belief that mistresses are slaves, his assumption that "to live familiarly with inferiors is degrading". Thus Rochester exposes for Jane the false economies of sexual systems which objectify women, either as wife or mistress: If Jane were "to become the successor of these poor girls, he would one day regard [her] with the same feeling". Sanctioned or illicit, heterosexual coupling is immoral in so far as it operates as a . . . construct requiring female inferiority and marginality. The old language of romance which inevitably tracks the genders in self-limiting, rigid, and eventually debilitating sexual roles constitutes a discourse of lies; the old romance about traditional marriage, about male dominance and female dependence, cannot be confused with the true story Jane tells. . . .

The ambitious wish for a story that would turn out differently shows itself in Jane's refusal to be either Rochester's mistress or St. John's unloved wife. Jane again *imposes her terms* on the received pattern and *affirms her power* in the face of a process already set in motion. . . .

Jane Has Fought but Not Completely Won

Autobiography is self-assertion: in order to speak her own narrative Jane must deny as temptation the self-abnegation which St. John recommends. . . . At first, Jane's needs for equity and purpose seem mechanically fulfilled by her financial independence and by Rochester's physical dependence. Yet these arbitrary stabs at equalization leave a tottering imbalance in Jane and Rochester's loving relationship. In one sense, Jane appropriates Rochester's narrative as she concludes her own: "He saw nature—he saw books through me; and never did I weary of gazing for his behalf, and of putting into words the effect of field, tree, town, river, cloud, sunbeam—of the landscape before us". Moreover, without qualification, Jane states that the intervening ten years of married life have brought "perfect concord". Yet below this apparent fulfillment resides the ambivalence and hesitancy palpable in their living at Ferndean, the estate Rochester earlier confesses is too unhealthy to house Bertha, and in their being withdrawn from society, without the stimulus of urban life Jane has long since desired.

Sexual Awakening
and Freedom

John Maynard

*John Maynard, a professor of English at New York University, is
the author of six books on Victorian literature and literary theory.
His books include* Charlotte Brontë and Sexuality.

*In the following excerpt, Maynard argues that Jane Eyre's struggle
for independence has a sexual context, beginning with her sexual
awakening at Thornfield Hall, Rochester's too-amorous advances
on her independence of mind, St. John's loveless proposition to
deprive her of independence, and, finally, her ability to have
both sexual passion with and independence from Rochester.
Sexuality is a vital part of the nature in which Jane sees her
Mother Earth. Rochester himself is associated with nature as are
the outdoor landscapes and gardens. The height of love and
sexual promise occurs in the garden on midsummer's eve. Jane's
letter to her relative saves her from a bigamist marriage and en-
sures her own financial independence. After she has left Thornfield Hall, she encounters threats to her selfhood and her passion.
St. John has no concept of selfhood, equality, or love. Only when
she returns to Rochester, does she feel fulfilled, not just as a
sexual woman, but a woman of independence.*

Jane's first battles, like the childhood battles of [her sister
Emily's novel] *Wuthering Heights*, have a primitive, heroic
quality that suggests an equation between childhood and the
primitive world of action. She stands up to her bullying cousin
and is felled only by superior force. She stands up to her aunt
Mrs Reed and in some sense wins her way out of that sup-
pression. At Lowood School she continues to play an active,

John Maynard, *Charlotte Bronte and Sexuality*. Cambridge University Press, 1984. ©
Cambridge University Press 1984. Reprinted with the permission of Cambridge University Press.

defiant role even as she undergoes the hero's education to patience and self-control from her mentors Helen Burns and Miss Temple. However much she learns from their placid acceptance of fate, from Helen's unworldly attendance on a better world, Jane remains the active, heroic figure. Her education amounts not to resignation but to a chastened activism—a resolution to pursue a new servitude if that is the best she can expect, but at least to pursue something.

Resisting Rochester's Encroachments

Thereafter the romance pattern is of course rewoven through the loom of a heroine's rather than hero's experience. In her main contest in life, the initial ambiguous relationship with Rochester and the temptation after the existence of his wife is revealed, Jane's heroic actions are all cast in the passive form necessary to a dependent female in the household of a rich man. Yet she remains the figure of romance heroism, fighting the dragon of custom and rank to claim her soul equality with Rochester on that midsummer's eve in the garden, asserting herself against Rochester's amorous encroachments on her independence, carrying through on her resolution to stage a Moscow retreat [like Napoléon from Russia] from Thornfield in her desolation after the discovery of Bertha. That central battle, the pathos in Jane's struggle toward fulfillment, ends in apparently total loss. All seems without hope; Jane's inability to conclude the contest at Thornfield by any mode but total retreat from fulfillment leaves her ironically caught in a sterile wasteland of her own devising. She seems bested, vanquished by the suppressive forces she has fought all her life but with which she must now collaborate.

The Prospect of Fulfillment
in a Flawed Eden

Finally the romance plot passes through tragic loss to Jane's recognition as a person endowed with family and loving relationships (as well as wealth) from which she has been alienated, not totally excluded. Despite the maiming that both she and Rochester have suffered in the main contest at Thornfield, Jane is granted final victory: at Ferndean, where the blinded and wounded Rochester has sequestered himself, she finds the green world of fulfillment in love that she has sought so long. As in more traditional romance structures, the ending does not entirely recapture an Eden outside the cycles of fruition and negation of the real world. Jane's progress as heroine leads her through early trials, to the seeming defeat at Thornfield, to final fulfillment; but romance improbabilities never elevate Jane's struggles above human needs or the possibility of loss. Ferndean has appropriately been called "a darkened and chastened Eden," a place where fulfillment is attained in full awareness of its enemies and possible loss. . . .

Nature as Symbol of Sexual Fulfillment

Structures that go beyond particular attributes of individual characters in *Jane Eyre* tend to derive from an implied author's vision of a natural world. If homage is paid by Jane to Helen Burns's unworldly piety or to God's ordinance in human affairs, the imagination of the novel is centered firmly in a world of nature. The use of landscape and natural images in the tales and the novelettes, good as that was, is here tremendously developed. . . . Rochester's vitality is imaged in honey bees or nesting birds. Sexual strength, and that strength as it threatens to become excessive, is colored in by images of brightness moving to fire itself. Fire is dangerous, yet its positive qualities of household warmth and human warmth predominate over its dangers. . . .

Growing things, trees and flowers, with their common and obvious sexual qualities, offer a continuous frame of reference in which all that is juicy, budding, or fruitful is preferred to what is juiceless, detached, barren. Jane begins life at the unnatural Gateshead looking on a lifeless, cold, rainy world and finding the same in her reading in Bewick. She finds death and barrenness at Lowood but also some promise of growth, reflected in her joy in her later free time among the flowers and low bushes. Jane first arrives at Thornfield in winter. What the implied author shows us in the beautiful description of nature in winter on that still evening when Jane first meets Rochester is the promise of fruition—of wild summer rose, of autumn nuts and blackberries—in the dried plant and seed of winter, an obvious but moving cognate with the sexual promise in the two future lovers. Natural growth proceeds apace with the growth of love, until when Jane returns from her visit to Gateshead she finds Rochester in a rich warm world of summer roses and hay-making. There follows the night of intense fruition of nature and feeling, the midsummer eve in Rochester's garden. . . .

From Elf to Woman

Narrative and plot structures, discussion of characters and discussion embodied in images all provide an orientation toward sexual values and experience. Brontë's primary focus is nonetheless on Jane. Within the world of sexual alternatives that she creates around her it is Jane's experience that is central. That experience is essentially a sexual *Bildung* [education] or prolonged rite of initiation. From the desolation and trauma of her youth, Jane is led suddenly and at a very early adult age (eighteen) into an emotionally intense and sexually charged relationship with an experienced and somewhat obsessive older man with all the glamour of worldly prosperity that she has been denied. . . .

Awakening the Passion of Womanhood

Jane denies that she feels jealousy of Blanche Ingram. When she sees her she finds her quite inferior to herself. Yet the effect of Rochester's manipulating trick is much as he wishes: Jane responds to the idea that he will marry Blanche and that she must find a position in John Bull's other island by standing up and asserting her equality with Rochester and, by implication, her superiority to Blanche. When Jane later berates Rochester for having tried to make her jealous, he doesn't so much answer her as point out his success. The suppressed underworld elf has emerged as a "fire-spirit" who "glowed in the cool moonlight" as she stood up and asserted her equality with Rochester.

That garden scene stands at the center of the novel and looks quite different depending on whether it is regarded from the front or the back. Looked at in relation to what goes before, it is a romantic culmination—more than many a novel or play offers as a symbol of happy sexual union. Jane not only asserts her equality with Rochester but is able, like Elizabeth Hastings, to resist what she misinterprets as an embrace from an engaged man. She asserts her love and balances it by being able to put her independence first when she finds it necessary. When he offers heart, hand, and a share of all his possessions, she is able to yield; she calls him Edward and they spend an evening cuddling together that culminates in a series of passionate kisses that are counterpointed by the force of the thunderstorm from which they flee....

Independence and Resolution

Jane's picaresque wandering and the romance discovery of her family when she appeals at a lonely house on the moors for rescue from the elements gives Brontë a looser, less intense and dramatic theater for her exploration of Jane. Unreal as the incidents are, they seem essentially appropriate to Jane's psychological needs. At Thornfield she has been driven back into a latent sexual state by internal and external influences; she has left under an intense compulsion that she does not consciously understand. Her wanderings then actually enact the process of her breakdown. Descending alone at a place called Whitcross, where, appropriately enough, she will undergo her ordeal, she commits herself to nature....

Brontë gives Jane forms of independence that establish her competence and authority quite apart from Rochester's power and wealth. She finds a poorly paying but responsible job as local schoolteacher in the town near her cousin's house. Then she is showered with riches that belong to her rather than Rochester. Astute readers see even this as a muted act of self-help because it was Jane herself who had written her uncle in the hope of receiving some financial support to make her relationship with Rochester less-uneven. The effect of her letter had been to send Bertha's brother back to stop the marriage as well as to direct the legacy to her. From this point of view, Jane prevented her own marriage in her quest for independence, then waited to secure it before returning to Rochester.

Jane's rehabilitation is marked by full internal studies at each extreme, first when Jane faces being on her own, then when she refuses to marry her cousin St John. In the first, Brontë interestingly studies Jane's emotional state as she faces her first night entirely on her own. She resolves to sleep by herself outside in the thick heath near where the coach dropped her off. Nature here becomes a substitute or symbol for the mother to whom a girl in Jane's position might normally return: "I have no relative but the universal mother, Nature: I will seek her breast and ask repose". In an almost grotesquely literal way, Jane snuggles up to nature's breast for the night and feeds herself on it by gathering bilberries. Buried in deep heath beside a protecting crag, head pillowed on a mossy swell, Jane's position is explicitly a running away from her sexual nature. She reports that she had a vague dread of intrusions on her solitude and these took decidedly masculine forms: "some sportsman or poacher" or "the rush of a bull". In her security from the kind of sexual intrusion that had pushed her so hard during her engagement and its aftermath, Jane is also able to accept her feelings more directly, less hypocritically. As she rests, she acknowledges gaping wounds, inward bleeding, riven chords. She admits to continued longing for him. Her heart, "impotent as a bird with both wings broken . . . still quivered its shattered pinions in vain attempts to seek him". As so often Brontë is excellent in finding the metaphorical language that embraces heart and passion at once. Jane feels both heart and sexuality cut out to impotence. She finds not merely a right arm cut off but both wings. Whatever harm she may be doing Rochester, she is suffering most emphatically herself. . . .

St. John's Threat to Selfhood

In St John, Jane finds a far more serious threat to her independence than any Rochester ever posed. St John will turn her sexual feelings in a totalitarian way to his own ends. She realizes as he presses his relentless suit upon her that she stands fair to be rushed "down the torrent of his will into the gulf of his existence" and there lose her own. With Rochester it was merely a matter of her being forced prematurely and even dishonestly to move in the direction her own will was naturally taking, toward sexual fulfillment with him. Jane never has Rochester out of her mind during her time at Moor House and Morton. Her frequent references show us how, despite the lack of any change in her perception of the impossibility of their relationship, her emotions are growing strongly and naturally back to him. Jane confesses that she has been possessed and tyrannized by "racking regrets" for her "broken idol and lost elysium". Brontë later gives a complex meditation, in the head of Jane at the time rather than Jane the narrator, in which she goes over most of the issues relating to Rochester. The meditation is in no way a schematic ordering that we can identify with the author. Instead we see Jane vacillating considerably as her emotions run in contrary directions. She thinks how much better off she is teaching school than being Rochester's mistress in a "silken snare" in some "southern clime, amongst the luxuries of a pleasure-villa". . . .

Jane Declares Love and Independence

Jane makes a point of her new status as well as her new attitude toward seeing Rochester. Her competitive feelings are now eased or eliminated altogether by her own success. Jane tells us how she rushed on from the ruins of Thornfield to Rochester's retreat at Ferndean in style, paying twice the price for a special trip. At Ferndean, she quickly will make herself at home as a lady, giving orders to her old friends the servants and generally taking over management. Jane will boast to Rochester that she is an independent woman. When he inquires how she can come by herself to him, she repeats: "I told you I am independent, sir, as well as rich: I am my own mistress". It is hard not to hear the implication: my own mistress, not yours. Her storybook wealth allows Jane to approach Rochester freely without the fears of a poor governess in the same situation. Some feminists might reasonably argue that her security, as unearned, is unreal; but it is as real as Rochester's and all those other confident male figures in English fiction who depend on inherited wealth for their social substantiality.

Jane also finds it easy to approach Rochester because his injuries make him, as she notes, dependent, just when she has become independent. Jane sees her main office in this reversal of role is not physical assistance but help in reviving his spirits: "it was not himself that could now kindle the lustre of animated expression: he was dependent on another for that office!". It makes Jane take the lead in their emotional relationship, as she does in virtually proposing to him.

In this way Brontë shows us a situation in which the disparity between Rochester and Jane has been evened out or even somewhat reversed. The book seems to suggest that such relative equality is a necessity for Jane's happy adjustment to loving Rochester.

Religion as a Tool
of Justification

Margaret Howard Blom

*Margaret Howard Blom taught at the University of British Co-
lumbia and published widely on the Brontës.*

*In this selection Blom states that Jane Eyre sees herself as not
only equal but also superior to other characters. She feels her
power over Rochester during their courtship. After the wedding
has been canceled, she realizes she must think first of herself and
say, "I care for myself." Her determination to survive ultimately
leads her to turn down St. John. Although Rochester often tried
to treat her as a doll, and St. John sees her as a soul on the edge
of damnation, the two men parallel one another in posing threats
to her selfhood. Rochester threatened her with passion, and St.
John threatens her with cold reason. Finally, she confronts everything and everyone who has attempted to deny her identity, including society and religion. Though she uses religion to justify
her decisions, she actually casts it aside, defying the religious dictate that women submit themselves to men. She is, writes Blom,
the epitome of modernity because she experiences the danger of
turning inward for authority and the glory of success.*

Jane's response to the disruption of the marriage ceremony
is, . . . as ambivalent as were her anticipatory visions of her
wedding. Her initial reaction is a despair so total that she lies
"faint; longing to be dead"; but as Rochester, who had patron-
ized and dominated her, becomes the suppliant and pleads for
her love, Jane's sleeping will revives. She has always sought not
just respect, but praise; not just equality, but superiority. Pride
and a sense of her preeminent merit led Jane to assert to her

aunt that far from being inferior to her cousins, "they are not fit to associate with me"; the same attitude led her to dismiss her rival—the beautiful, well-born Blanche Ingram—as being "a mark beneath jealousy: she was too inferior to excite the feeling". This same sense of her own worth at first controlled Jane's response to Rochester; but when she demanded in Thornfield's garden that he see her as his 'equal', her own overwhelming love for him had itself rendered her inferior and incapable of pressing her claim. Now the situation is reversed, and she sees that she has at least "the passing second of time . . . in which to control and restrain him. . . . I felt an inward power; a sense of influence, which supported me. The crisis was perilous; but not without its charm".

Jane Puts Herself First

The moment will, as Jane clearly sees, decide her destiny. Rochester, who insists that "to live familiarly with inferiors is degrading" and who asserts, "I now hate the recollection of the time I passed with Céline, Giacinta, and Clara," begs Jane to become his mistress since he cannot make her his wife. Jane knows that if she assents to becoming "the successor of these poor girls, he would one day regard me with the same feeling which now in his mind desecrated their memory"; for during the last weeks as she began "mechanically to obey him", she has, like them, become a mere puppet, a doll—a plaything to be cast aside when play is done.

The terms in which she couches her refusal to become his mistress are highly significant: she refuses not out of obedience to "Conscience" or "Reason," for they "turned traitors against me, and charged me with crime in resisting him"; she refuses not because she has ceased to love him, for "feeling" "clamoured wildly," saying, "Oh, comply". Rather, she remains adamant in her rejection of Rochester's plea because of her steadfast belief that in this ultimate crisis her own needs are superior to all other demands, that they justify even her decision to function as "the instrument of evil to what [she] wholly love[s]". She thus decides to abandon her lover to what she knows will be "misery" and to what she fears will be "ruin" on the grounds that she must obey that "indomitable" inner voice which insists, "I care for myself. The more solitary, the more friendless, the more unsustained I am, the more I will respect myself". To his anguished cry, "Oh, Jane, this is bitter! This—this is wicked. It would not be wicked to love me," she coldly responds, "It would to obey you".

Self-Preservation

Jane's flight in the middle of the night saves her from psychological destruction, but it does not lead to her happiness and safety. Rather, her panicked flight from the temptation she continues to feel and fear is a negative move that commits her to an existence as perilous as the one she flees. At Moor House, she comes to see how cold repression of all feeling results only in spiritual imprisonment, the end of which is destruction. She finds that under St. John's influence, her mind becomes a "rayless dungeon", and she realizes that the man whose "Christianity covers human deformity" "could soon kill [her]".

Jane's struggle to maintain her independence when she is threatened by St. John's powerful will parallels her battle against Rochester. The two men represent the antithetical forces of passion and reason which exist within Jane; therefore, part of her nature spontaneously responds to each. Jane fully realizes that Rochester and St. John see her differently and wish to wed her for different reasons but that, despite these differences, they both seek to destroy her selfhood. Rochester—who believes her to be innocent and pure—wishes to force her to function as his "better self," his "good angel". St. John—who believes she is in danger of becoming a spiritual "castaway" and a "vessel of wrath" doomed to "perdition"— wishes to save her endangered soul, thus carrying out the directive of Christ his master and, at the same time, winning a "useful tool" which he can wield for the glory of God. . . .

Using Religion as Justification

The grounds on which Jane ultimately rejects the demands of St. John are the same as those on which she denied the commands of Rochester: in both cases, she steadfastly asserts that her own needs must take precedence over all other considerations. Clearly, despite her habitual and characterizing use of the conventional language of Christianity, Jane is not motivated by a Christian concern to save her soul by submitting her will to God's. Instead, she uses religion to justify following the self-seeking course to which she is already committed. She rationalizes her decision to leave Rochester by insisting that she must "keep the law given by God; sanctioned by man"; but when St. John—whose "sternness" is that of "the warrior Great-heart"—speaks, she refuses to obey, although at the very moment, "Religion called—Angels beckoned—God commanded".

Despite the fact that at this climactic moment, she believes she is deciding the fate of her soul and feels that "for safety and bliss [in eternity], all here might be sacrificed in a second", she hesitates to make the sacrifice demanded of her and acts at last only when the answer to her prayer for guidance is the one she wants to hear—the voice of Rochester calling her back to him. Her immediate triumph over St. John's power is stated in terms which confirm Jane's sense of the absolute correctness of her own inner drives and her total confidence in her ability to assert her will:

> I broke from St. John. . . . It was *my* time to assume ascendancy. *My* powers were in play, and in force. . . . Where there is energy to command well enough, obedience never fails. I mounted to my chamber; . . . fell on my knees; and prayed in my way—a different way to St. John's, but effective in its own fashion. I seemed to penetrate very near a

Mighty Spirit. . . . I rose . . .—took a resolve—and lay down, unscared, enlightened—eager but for the daylight. . . .

Jane's Mastery

The conclusion of the novel thus chronicles the totality of Jane's triumph over all that has threatened and opposed her will—society, St. John, Rochester, religion—and illuminates the gravity of the decision she has made. The last words of *Jane Eyre* are devoted not to Rochester and to Jane's domestic bliss, but to a summary of St. John's career as a "high master-spirit, which aims to fill a place in the first rank of those who are redeemed from the earth . . . who are called, and chosen, and faithful". At the crisis of her relationship with St. John, Jane refuses this call to service and redemption. . . .

Defiant and Without Religion

Almost from the day of its first publication, readers have argued over the nature of the morality and the quality of the religious thought in *Jane Eyre*. Charlotte acknowledged herself "distressed" by a contemporary review which insisted that Jane "is the personification of an unregenerate and undisciplined spirit" and that her strength "is the strength of a mere heathen mind which is a law unto itself." Yet a close reading of the novel seems to support this view. Given the fact that ultimately and triumphantly Jane achieves not only what her own spirit demands but what her maimed lover comes to desire, it is difficult to believe that Charlotte, with her extensive knowledge of Christian doctrine and her familiarity with both [poet John] Milton and the Bible, was unaware that the situation in which she finally placed her heroine not only celebrates Jane's decision to be governed solely by her own will but reverses the traditional Christian view of the superiority of men over women.

The perverse echo of [Milton's epic poem] *Paradise Lost* is explicit: Eve entered upon her temptation doomed to fall by her insistence on independence from Adam, her "best Prop," but the blind and maimed Rochester leans upon Jane, who has become "both his prop and guide". Jane has always insisted on being the center of her own world; she is now also the center of Rochester's. God has been removed from his throne, and Jane reigns supreme. The chastened Rochester whom Jane finds at Ferndean insists he has acknowledged the existence of supernatural power, has repented his past life, and has sought to reform himself in accordance with Christian principles; but in truth, Rochester worships only Jane—he has "supplicated God, that if it seemed good to Him, I might soon be taken from this life, and admitted to that world to come, where there was still hope of rejoining Jane", and his only verbalized prayer is limited to the single word which is "the alpha and omega of [his] heart's wishes": "Jane! Jane! Jane!". Hearing him speak of this invocation which calls her back, Jane implicitly equates herself with the Virgin Mary, saying, "I kept these things then, and pondered them in my heart" [see Luke 2:51]. So Jane remains consistent to the end: her "sweetest wishes", which have been so totally fulfilled, are, as the condition of her world demands, selfish wishes. . . .

A critical evaluation of *Jane Eyre* is in one sense made unnecessary, if not presumptuous, by the fact that generations of readers have established Jane as one of the characters of English literature who have attained virtually mythic proportions. Charlotte Brontë's story of a plain orphan girl whose superior qualities are finally acknowledged and who gains the reward of love and power has become the modern version of the Cinderella tale; for Jane not only wins her Prince Charming but does so by steadfastly asserting her independence, becoming thereby not merely his consort but his queen. . . .

Split between the wish to remain safely passive and the need to indulge in the excitement of rebellion; approving the severely rational, yet delighting and trusting in intuition, imagination, and vision; desiring sexual satisfaction, yet fear-ing passion—Jane is not only a fictionalized version of her creator but the very epitome of modern mankind, who, having chosen to turn inward for authority, finds only ambivalence and confusion. In her struggles to wrest safety, comfort, and love from her hostile environment, Jane encounters the dangers of our nightmares; in her success, she realizes our dreams.

Class Restrictions on Jane's Independence

Terry Eagleton

Terry Eagleton, professor of English at the Lancaster University in England, is considered a pioneer in the field of literary theory and a top critic. He has published more than forty books.

Eagleton explains in this selection that Jane Eyre *is a contradiction of smoldering passion and control; rebellion and social order; romance and pragmatism. Passion and romance must continually be controlled to keep them from obliterating the self. But death and lovelessness can also kill the spirit, as Jane knows in listening to St. John Rivers's demands. At first she is prepared to go with him as a missionary but not yield herself to him in marriage. Jane has no kindred to advise and care for her as she grows up. The resulting deep loneliness gives her some freedom. She can later secure independence and choose Rochester as a true kinsman after having erased the "second-hand kin"—the oppressive Reeds—from her life.*

Where Charlotte Brontë differs most from Emily [Brontë] is precisely in . . . [the] impulse to negotiate passionate self-fulfilment on terms which preserve the social and moral conventions intact, and so preserve intact the submissive, enduring, everyday self which adheres to them. Her protagonists are an extraordinarily contradictory amalgam of smouldering rebelliousness and prim conventionalism, gushing Romantic fantasy and canny hard-headedness, quivering sensitivity and blunt rationality. It is, in fact, a contradiction closely related to their roles as governesses or private tutors. The governess is a servant, trapped within a rigid social function which demands

Terry Eagleton, *Myths of Power: A Marxist Study of the Brontës*. Palgrave, 2005. © Terry Eagleton 1975, 1988, 2005. All rights reserved. Reproduced with permission of Palgrave Macmillan.

industriousness, subservience and self-sacrifice; but she is also an 'upper' servant, and so (unlike, supposedly, other servants) furnished with an imaginative awareness and cultivated sensibility which are precisely her stock-in-trade as a teacher. . . .

Yielding

To allow passionate imagination premature rein is to be exposed, vulnerable and ultimately self-defeating: it is to be locked in the red room, enticed into bigamous marriage, ensnared . . . in a hopelessly self-consuming love. Passion springs from the very core of the self and yet is hostile, alien, invasive; the world of internal fantasy must therefore be locked away, as the mad Mrs Rochester stays locked up on an upper floor of Thornfield, slipping out to infiltrate the 'real' world only in a few unaware moments of terrible destructiveness. The inner world must yield of necessity to the practical virtues of caution, tact and observation . . .—the wary, vigilant virtues by which the self's lonely integrity can be defended in a spying, predatory society, a society on the watch for the weak spot which will surrender you into its hands. The Romantic self must be persistently recalled to its deliberately narrowed and withered definition of rationality. 'Order! No snivel!—no sentiment!—no regret! I will endure only sense and resolution', whispers Jane Eyre to herself, fixing her errant thoughts on the hard fact that her relationship with Rochester is of a purely cash-nexus kind. . . .

Refusing Loveless Convention and Illicit Passion

Jane . . . must refuse Rivers as she has refused Rochester: loveless conventionalism and illicit passion both threaten the kind of fulfilment the novel seeks for her. Yet of course Rivers represents more than mere convention. In his fusion of disciplined aloofness and restless desire he is an extreme version of Jane herself, akin to her in more than blood; and he is acute enough to spot the affinity: 'for in your nature is an alloy as detrimental to repose as that in mine; though of a different kind'. The difference, however, is what finally counts. It is true that Jane finds Rivers's restlessness intriguing as well as alarming: the 'frequent flash and changeful dilation of his eye', his 'troubling impulses of insatiate yearnings and disquieting aspirations', evoke crucial aspects of herself at the same time as they recall Rochester's engaging moodiness. Indeed, Rivers's repressed love for Rosamund Oliver is a cruder, more agonised version of Rochester's own early enigmatic relationship with Jane. Yet Rivers is a frigid as well as a Romantic figure, and for Jane to accept him would mean disastrous compromise. 'I daily wished more to please him: but to do so, I felt daily more and more that I must disown half my nature, stifle half my faculties, wrest my tastes from their original bent, force myself to the adoption of pursuits for which I had no natural vocation.' . . .

Dependency and Rivers

Rivers's demands, indeed, pull in precisely the opposite direction to Rochester's. He threatens to uproot you lovelessly from idyllic settlement to an *unpleasantly* foreign world, and to a life with no determinate end but death. Jane is certainly willing at times to trade settlement for independence: much as she finds the soft domesticity of the Rivers girls seductive, she is quick to tell St John that she wants an income of her own. In India, however, she would have the worst of all worlds: homelessness, lovelessness and subjugation. She rejects Rivers not only because his demands violate her identity, but because of his imperious masculinity. In India she would be 'at his side always, and always restrained, and always checked—forced to keep the fire of [her] nature continually low, to compel it to burn inwardly and never utter a cry, though the imprisoned flame consume vital after vital'. Far from combining the excitingly exotic with the lovably familiar, India for Jane would be a mixture of the alien and the over-close. Charlotte's hero-ines, as we shall see, habitually welcome male domination as a stimulant to their fiery natures; but Rivers's despotism would be merely oppressive. Jane, then, is willing to accompany him to India if she may go free: 'I will give the missionary my en-ergies—it is all he wants—but not myself: that would be only adding the husk and shell to the kernel. For them he has no use: I retain them'. Scathingly inverting the husk-kernel image, Jane accepts the social role of missionary only if she can pre-serve unbetrayed the authentic self which belongs to Roches-ter; and this is hardly a constructive advance on the schizoid condition she has endured for most of her life. Rivers offers a social function which involves the sacrifice of personal fulfil-ment; Rochester's offer involves exactly the opposite. Both are inferior propositions to becoming Mrs Rochester, at once a fulfilling personal commitment and an enviable public role. . . .

Purchased at Great Price

Jane flippantly denies that her return to Rochester involves any sort of martyrdom ('Sacrifice! What do I sacrifice? Famine for food, expectation for content'), and of course she is right; but besides forestalling our own mixed feelings about Jane's fairy-tale triumph by saying it for us, the comment is meant to alert us to the real deprivations she has endured, and so obviate any sense that she has won her self-fulfilment on the cheap. Jane and Rochester are also martyrs in their own suc-cessful way; and in this sense the final unbanishable image of Rivers is less a critique of their conjugal happiness than a symbol of the suffering they underwent to achieve it—the pa-tron saint, as it were, of the marriage. It is convenient to leave Rivers with the last word when the genuine threat he repre-sents has been nullified. . . .

Without Family One Is Lonely and Free

At the centre of all Charlotte's novels, . . . is a figure who ei-ther lacks or deliberately cuts the bonds of kinship. This leaves the self a free, blank, 'pre-social' atom: free to be injured and exploited, but free also to progress, move through the class-structure, choose and forge relationships, strenuously utilise its talents in scorn of autocracy or paternalism. The novels are deeply informed by this bourgeois ethic, but there is more to be said than that. For the social status finally achieved by the ... self is at once meritoriously won and inherently proper. Jane's uncle is said to be a tradesman, and the Reeds despise her for it; but Bessie comments that the Eyres were as much gentry as the Reeds, and her Rivers cousins have an impressively ancient lineage. Rochester seems a grander form of gentry, and Jane's relationship with him is of course socially unequal; but it is, nevertheless, a kind of returning home as well as an enviable move upwards. Given relationships are certainly constrictive: they mediate a suave violence deep-seated in society itself, as John Reed's precociously snobbish remark suggests. But knowing where you genetically belong still counts for a good deal in the end. Charlotte's fiction portrays the unprotected self in its lonely conquest of harsh conditions, and so intimates a meritocratic vision; but individualist self-reliance leads you to roles and relations which are objectively fitting.

Jane, then, disowns what second-hand kin she has, caring never to see the Reeds again, surviving instead by her own talents; she creates the relationships which matter, those of spiritual rather than blood affinity. ('I believe [Rochester] is of mine;—I am sure he is,—I feel akin to him ... though rank and wealth sever us widely. I have something in my brain and heart, in my blood and nerves, that assimilates me mentally to him. ...

Jane's Ambivalence About the Lower Class

Jane is furious with the Reeds because they treat her as a servant when she isn't one; her smouldering hatred of their snobbery is thus shot through with shared class-assumptions about

Mr. Rochester wears expensive clothing while Jane wears plain, common clothes showing the class differences in the film version of Jane Eyre. *Picture Post/Stringer/Hulton Archive/ Getty Images.*

the poor. ('No; I should not like to belong to poor people.') Her response to the pupils at Morton school is similarly double-edged: distasteful though she finds their unmannerliness, she 'must not forget that these coarsely-clad little peasants are of flesh and blood as good as the scions of the gentlest genealogy; and that the germs of native excellence, refinement, intelligence, kind feeling, are as likely to exist in their hearts as in those of the best born'. The demotic generosity of this is sharply qualified by that stern self-reminder; Jane's doctrine of spiritual equality stems logically from her own experience, but it has to fight hard against the social discriminations bred into an expensively clad child. (Her egalitarian defence of the 'British peasantry' is based, ironically, on a dogma of chauvinist superiority: they are at least preferable to their 'ignorant, coarse, and besotted' European counterparts.) Jane feels degraded by her role as schoolmistress ('I had taken a step which sank instead of raising me in the scale of social existence'), but guiltily scorns the feeling as 'idiotic'; and that tension deftly defines the petty-bourgeois consciousness which clings to real class-distinctions while spiritually rejecting them. She is, for instance, priggishly quick to point out to the Rivers' servant Hannah that she may be a beggar but at least she is a high-class one. . . .

Jane's relationship with Rochester is marked by these ambiguities of equality, servitude and independence. He himself conceives of the union in terms of spiritual equality: '"My bride is here", he said, again drawing me to him, "because my equal is here, and my likeness. Jane, will you marry me?"' Far from offering a radically alternative ethic, spiritual equality is what actually smooths your progress through the class-system: Rochester may be spiritually egalitarian but he is still socially eligible. Jane is on the whole submissive to social hierarchy but shares her master's view that spiritual qualities count for more: she has no hesitation in dismissing Blanche Ingram as inferior to herself. She wants a degree of independence in marriage—'"It would indeed be a relief", I thought, "if I had ever so small an independency"'—but it is, significantly, 'small': she can hope to bring Rochester an accession of fortune but hardly to get on genuinely equal terms. Independence, then, is an intermediate position between complete equality and excessive docility: it allows you freedom, but freedom within a proper deference.

When stung to righteous anger, Jane can certainly claim a fundamental human equality with her employer: 'Do you think, because I am poor, obscure, plain, and little, I am soulless and heartless?' There are, in fact, reasons other than simple humanitarian ones why Jane and Rochester are not as socially divided as may at first appear. Rochester, the younger son of an avaricious landed gentleman, was denied his share in the estate and had to marry instead into colonial wealth; Jane's colonial uncle dies and leaves her a sizeable legacy, enough for independence. The colonial trade which signified a decline in status for Rochester signifies an advance in status for Jane, so that although they are of course socially unequal, their fortunes spring from the same root. Yet Jane does not finally claim equality with Rochester; the primary terms on which Charlotte Brontë's fiction handles relationships are those of dominance and submission. The novels dramatise a society in which almost all human relationships are power-struggles; and because 'equality' therefore comes to be defined as equality of power, it is an inevitably complicated affair. . . .

The Desire to Dominate

This complex blend is a recurrent feature of relationships in the novels. Charlotte's protagonists want independence, but they also desire to dominate; and their desire to dominate is matched only by their impulse to submit to a superior will. The primary form assumed by this ambiguity is a sexual one: the need to venerate and revere, but also to exercise power, enacts itself both in a curious rhythm of sexual attraction and antagonism, and in a series of reversals of sexual roles. The maimed and blinded Rochester, for example, is in an odd way even more 'masculine' than he was before (he is 'brown', 'shaggy', 'metamorphosed into a lion'), but because he is helpless he is also 'feminine'; and Jane, who adopts a traditionally feminine role towards him ('It is time some one undertook to rehumanise you'), is thereby forced into the male role of protectiveness. She finds him both attractive and ugly, as he finds her both plain and fascinating. Rochester's lack of conventional good looks, in contrast to Rivers's blandly classical features, reflects his idiosyncratic roughness and so underlines his male mastery, but it also makes him satisfyingly akin to Jane herself. Blanche Ingram is a 'beauty', but her aggressive masculinity contrasts sharply with Jane's pale subduedness; her dominative nature leads her to desire a husband who will be a foil rather than a rival to her, but it also prompts her to despise effeminate men and admire strong ones:

> 'I grant an ugly *woman* is a blot on the fair face of creation; but as to the *gentlemen,* let them be solicitous to possess only strength and valour: let their motto be:—Hunt, shoot and fight: the rest is not worth a fillip. Such should be my device, were I a man.'

> 'Whenever I marry,' she continued, after a pause which none interrupted, 'I am resolved my husband shall not be a rival, but a foil to me. I will suffer no competitor near the throne; I shall exact an undivided homage; his devotions shall not be shared between me and the shape he sees in his mirror.'

The arrogance of this, of course, counts heavily against Blanche; it is hardly likely to charm the listening Rochester. Jane, who shares Blanche's liking for 'devilish' men, knows better than she does how they are to be handled—when to exert her piquant will and when to be cajolingly submissive....

Revenge Against an Oppressive Order

This simultaneity of attraction and antagonism, reverence and dominance, is relevant to a more general ambiguity about power which pervades Charlotte's fiction. It parallels and embodies the conflicting desires of the oppressed outcast for independence, for passive conformity to a secure social order, and for avenging self-assertion over that order. Revenge does not, in fact, seem too strong a word for what happens at the end of *Jane Eyre*. Jane's repressed indignation at a dominative society, prudently allowed back throughout the book, is finally released—not by Jane herself, but by the novelist; and the victim is the symbol of that social order, Rochester. The crippled Rochester is the novel's sacrificial offering to social convention, to Jane's subconscious hostility and, indeed, to her own puritan guilt; by satisfying all three demands simultaneously, it allows her to adopt a suitably subjugated role while experiencing a fulfilling love and a taste of power.... In the end, the outcast bourgeois achieves more than a humble place at the fireside: she also gains independence vis-à-vis the upper class, and the right to engage in the process of taming it. The worldly Rochester has already been purified by fire; it is now for Jane to rehumanise him. By the device of an ending, bourgeois initiative and genteel settlement, sober rationality and Romantic passion, spiritual equality and social distinction, the actively affirmative and the patiently deferential self, can be merged into mythical unity.

Revolution with an Undertone of Conservatism

Parama Roy

Parama Roy, who has written extensively on manorial society in England, is associate professor of English at the University of California–Davis.

Jane Eyre *is a mixture of conservative and revolutionary thought, writes Roy in this selection. The novel was excoriated in its day as violently anti-Christian, and it has been adopted by many readers as a revolutionary text with regard to women's issues of equality and independence. Roy sees it as a radical novel that is "qualified" by a conservative subtext. On the radical side, Brontë undermines the aristocratic country manor, and the society it epitomizes, as sordid, dark, and destructive. By the end, however, Jane has joined the propertied master class and assumed faith in a religion she has questioned since childhood (when she replied to Brocklehurst that the best way to keep from going to hell is to live long and not die.) Jane had from young girlhood sought intellectual liberty and refuses to participate in Thornfield Hall's social games. She flees Rochester, Roy contends, because she is following social conventions and traditional religion. Her later inheritance also seems to soften her rebellious views.*

When *Jane Eyre* was released to the British reading public in 1847, it was anathematized by Lady Eastlake, among others, as an "anti-Christian composition." In our own time, it has been sacralized as a handbook for feminists and revolutionaries, articulating all the rage of the unaccommodated and dispossessed. But contemporary adulation of Brontë the radical feminist often overlooks the tenacity of her Tory [conser-

Parama Roy, *Studies in English Literature, 1500-1900*, vol. 29, Autumn 1989. Copyright © William Marsh Rice University, 1989. Reproduced by permission.

vative] convictions, which inform even *Jane Eyre*, arguably one of the most unorthodox of her novels. It is true that Brontë endeavors to inaugurate in *Jane Eyre* a new and different discourse about the structures of power in nineteenth-century England. In particular, she purports to reevaluate, and indeed to arraign in no uncertain terms, the hegemony of property and male power as reified in the manorial ethos and in the religious establishment. To this end, she borrows extensively from various and widely different subgenres—the novel of social protest, the spiritual autobiography, feminist discourse, and, naturally traditional manorial literature. . . . What emerges ultimately is not a dialectic between different orders of value, but a radical text which is qualified in significant ways by a conservative subtext.

The radicalism of the text is simple enough to establish, particularly in the departures it makes from the norms for country-house literature. . . . In traditional accounts of manorial life, the country-house world is experienced and assessed by a protagonist who belongs to that world and participates in it. But in *Jane Eyre* the country house is viewed and judged from the outside. The teller of the tale is a governess, a gentleman's daughter certainly, but, by her own definition, "disconnected, poor, and plain." . . . In addition to being dislocated from the great house by her poverty and rank, Jane is distanced from it by being female, and she rejects it as inadequate for her happiness. Brontë in fact spurns the civic and political role of the great house; in *Jane Eyre* the great house has ceased almost altogether to exist in a public dimension. . . . Country-house concerns like power, primogeniture, inheritance, and "suitable" alliances are exposed as shabby and destructive. Indeed, the great house—whether it be Gateshead or Thornfield—has become the locus of innumerable oppressions. Brontë's protagonists must ultimately flee to Ferndean, that place in the woods where the oppositions between "nature" and man-made spaces no longer exist.

The Conservative Impulse

However, the radical character of Brontë's assertions is confused, paralyzed, occasionally even subverted by some of the text's immanent contradictions. The astringency and power of Brontë's crusade against the manorial ethos and its valorization of property and patriarchalism is neutralized to some degree at least by the astonishing somersaults of a plot that converts Jane from one of the disinherited to one of the propertied; Jane ends up rather too well-adjusted and well-endowed for Brontë to carry through her radical convictions to the end. Brontë gives her assent to camouflaged and insidious forms of patriarchalism in other ways as well. She canonizes the self-mortifying and meek Helen Burns, the apologist for Brocklehurst and for the status quo; she approves Rochester's summary and callous treatment of his West Indian wife; and she is manifestly enthusiastic about the exploitation of colonized peoples. She thus yields a furtive assent to the authoritative word of her culture, in matters socioeconomic as well as religious. Ultimately, as we shall see, these mandates are very similar in kind, so that Jane's submission to the religious proscriptions ordained by her society, in the instance of her flight from Rochester, and in her beatification of Helen Burns and St. John, is of a piece with her stealthy acquiescence in the economic and class values of her society. . . .

Jane Challenges and Accepts
Conventional Christianity

Yet, despite all the idealization bestowed upon her, Helen seems too much at ease in Zion; in a situation that clearly demands outrage and resistance, she reacts with a degree of meekness, indeed moral slothfulness, that implicates her in the oppressions of John Reed and Brocklehurst and their tribe. . . . Her formula for coping with injustice also seems more pragmatic and appropriate: "When we are struck at without a reason, we should strike back again very hard; I am sure we should—so hard as to teach the person who struck us never to do it again". We know by now that it is precisely Jane's strong sense of her own rights, her indignation at injustice, and her willingness to rebel that have liberated her from Gateshead. But Helen responds to Jane's remark by saying (with Brontë's approval, it is impossible to doubt), "Heathens and savage tribes hold that doctrine; but Christians and civilised nations disown it". The remark appears to anticipate Brontë's consideration, much later in the novel, of Christianity's paternalistic, "civilizing" mission among "heathen and savage tribes"—a mission that, most appropriately, is undertaken by St. John. Helen is a kind friend to Jane, but her quietist philosophy, with its "alloy of inexpressible sadness," is hardly adequate for those who wish to "keep in good health, and not die." . . .

With Miss Temple's departure, Jane disavows all the passivity that she had imitated in her monitress and becomes her old self: "my mind had put off all it had borrowed of Miss Temple. . . . I desired liberty."

The desire for liberty leads Jane directly to Thornfield Hall, the central abode in her history. . . .

Country-house norms and values are thus quite overtly rejected in *Jane Eyre*. Jane and Rochester are both victims of the conventions of the English landed class—he by virtue of being an insider, she (as we have seen) by virtue of being an outsider. It may not unreasonably be argued that Rochester's miseries and corruption stem from his subservience to the demands of his station. His wife Bertha, whose marriage to him is arranged to ensure his financial status as a son of a great house, is a symbol of all that is diseased, limiting, and hateful about the country-house world. The charades played out in Thornfield are the most obvious emblem of the roles the country-house world forces on the individual. Rochester is obviously the supreme actor. Wedded by the contingencies of his station to a mad wife, he enacts a variety of roles designed to protect the secret of the house. Blanche Ingram participates aggressively in socially approved and disingenuous games, and so do all the other members of the house party. Only Jane, houseless and alien, remain consistent with herself. . . .

Religious Contradictions

Each experience transforms Jane into a "cold, solitary girl"; the images of frost, storm, cold, and ice that had defined the landscapes of Gateshead are once more evoked. Like Gateshead, Thornfield proves inadequate to provide an ideal of felicitous space.

So Jane leaves Thornfield and its master, invoking as she leaves the Christian sanctions against uncovenanted sexual relations. This has proved to be a highly vexatious problem for readers of the novel from [nineteenth-century feminist author] George Eliot on. Jane does not leave because she cannot condone Rochester's deception—that would have been easy enough to understand; she leaves because she will not live with him as his mistress. Why, it may be asked, has Brontë suddenly introduced a grammar of religious motivations in a novel that has hitherto celebrated departures from normative values? And why has Jane adopted the ideology of that most unpleasant of patriarchs, Brocklehurst? In Gateshead, Jane's refusal to be a self-effacing Victorian child, and her use of the tabooed instrument of rebellion had freed her from an oppressive situation; her dissatisfaction with the narrow Lowood life had exposed her to the wider possibilities of happiness at Thornfield; and she had recognized that to suppress her unorthodox love for a gentleman of the landed class would be a "blasphemy against nature." Her affiliations in the struggle between Nature and Grace have always been evident; "Grace" has hitherto been only another name for social subjugation. . . .

Jane's Religious Reasons
for Leaving Rochester

If the act of leaving Rochester is a form of regression or a clever stratagem, then what are we to make of Jane's prayers during her exile on the moors, her conviction of the providence of God, and, above all, of Rochester's repentance and acceptance of faith? These cannot be rationalized in the same terms. Jane's flight has alternatively been explained as the outcome of her fears—never fully articulated even to herself—of being dominated, physically, emotionally, and financially, by her lover. This reading of Jane's apparently erratic motivations is an impressive one, and it certainly validates the structural necessity of the Moor House section. But even this is not a completely satisfying explanation. The most emphatically feminist reading of the event cannot dissipate the specifically religious terms in which Jane couches her decision to leave Rochester ("I will keep the law given by God; sanctioned by man"), and the *religious* (not feminist) nature of Rochester's conversion. It is not simply that he accepts Jane as his equal and his helpmate in the Ferndean section; he also "[begins] to see and acknowledge the hand of God in [his] doom." . . .

It seems to me an indisputable instance of her submission to cultural practices; it is also a suggestive prelude to her endorsement (later in the novel) of the country-house values she had earlier decried. Religious proscriptions and economic and class values mandated by her society win a kind of covert acquiescence from her; and thus the implicit moral thesis of the earlier part of the novel is at least partially contradicted. . . .

But there is an additional dimension to Jane's acquisition of wealth: it changes her from one of the dispossessed to one of the class of owners that she has always despised. Something is at odds here with the governess's passionate assertion of equality with the wealthy landed gentleman. There is something a little distasteful too in her snobbish emphasis on her family's gentility and ancient respectability. Jane has always been portrayed as the social outcast who is, by virtue of her very Otherness, superior to the world of the great house. Her discovery of wealth reverses that to a certain degree.

The cottage, valorized as the locus of tranquility and guiltlessness, is contrasted with the corruptions of the great house and the metropolis. Ferndean, though, has a more explicitly reclusive character than the cottage of Victorian ideal. The cottage never exists in an unpeopled landscape. The Princess of [poet Alfred Lord] Tennyson's "Palace of Art" descends to a cottage in the vale in order to escape solitude. Ferndean, on the other hand, with its narrow door and narrow windows, repels almost all contact with the world. Even Diana and Mary Rivers do not enter the sanctum more than once a year.

We find therefore that even at the end of the novel, the protagonist is only marginally assimilated; and Rochester detaches himself, it would appear, from the duties of a squire. The figure of the alienated protagonist is thus occasionally used by Brontë as a means of chastising the country-house world. Jane the unassimilable outsider is generally worthier than those in positions of social power, whether it be the Reeds, the guests at Rochester's house party, the fabulously wealthy Masons, St. John, or even her lover.

But Brontë's criticism of things as they are, especially things as they are among the landed, housed, and powerful members of the world of the great house, is diluted considerably by Jane's latter-day assumption of wealth and gentility; it is also confused by the rather smug theodicy of the last section that can cheerfully see Rochester's terrible sufferings as an aspect of divine mercy. Brontë's insidious concessions to the socioeconomic and religious imperatives she had begun by condemning neutralizes the causticity of her invective against the orthodoxies of the manorial and the religious establishments. The final chapter, which details the retreat to Ferndean as well as the "heroism" and impending martyrdom of St. John, is a wonderfully apposite example of the novel's mixed impulses. All engagement with the world (and the great house was very emphatically a symbol of engagement with the world) is rejected in the move to Ferndean. Traditionally a place to come home to ..., it is here a place to be fled. On the other hand, there is the extraordinary paean to St. John that closes the narrative. The sanitization and glorification of the missionary—a development that has astonished and disconcerted most readers—seems to me to be one more instance of Brontë's uneasy accommodation with the Victorian religious superego. It is difficult to deny that her decision to allow St. John literally the last word is ideologically loaded and that it emblematizes most aptly her clandestine submission to the dictates of the institutions she had sought to reevaluate and dislocate.

Contemporary Perspectives on Female Independence

Finding Independence and Embracing Feminism

Rosanna Eang

At publication time, Rosanna Eang was a medical student at Ohio University.

In the following viewpoint, Eang, a daughter of Cambodian immigrants, remembers the extreme poverty she survived as a child in a culture that demeaned women. This marked her life forever, just as Jane Eyre can never rid her mind of the Red Room. But Rosanna had the advantage of a mother who exemplified "woman power," counter to her culture. She explains the outrage and shock of her Cambodian relatives at her and her sisters' journey toward independence, feminism, and traditionally all-male professions. It is, ironically, her defiant mother, always required to be dependent in her culture, who fights for her daughters' fulfillment.

Poverty has a staggering effect on the lives of women and children, stripping away human dignity. My own experiences of poverty as well as my mother's example of strength and resilience in the face of great odds have shaped my outlook on leadership and activism as well as my career goals. This is a story about my mother, my life, and my passionate pursuit of helping women and children living in poverty.

Poverty and Lack of Choice

In November of 1981 my parents, two brothers, sister, grandpa, aunts, uncles, and cousins first arrived in America, in the City of Brotherly Love, after they had fled three years of civil war and starvation in their home country of Cambodia. The brutal genocide of the Pol Pot Khmer Rouge regime had taken more than one million lives, including those of many of my aunts and uncles as well as my grandparents. My father became a monk at nineteen and lived in the temple for five years before he left. He and my mother had an arranged marriage, which is customary in Cambodian traditions. My mother and father are actually first cousins, which is also quite common. My father was twenty-five and my mother twenty-three when they were married in their rural town of Poom Peanne, Cambodia. Although my mother was pregnant eleven times, she has only five surviving children. She gave birth to her eldest son when she was twenty-four. My second brother was born seven years later, a few years before the war began, and my older sister was born during the war. My family is only here today because of my mother's determination. During the war in Cambodia, she kept my two older brothers and sister alive while my father went into hiding because the Khmer Rouge was executing all the men who were educated or were formerly monks. My mother and siblings slept in jungles along the mountainsides, and my mother used her machete to hunt for food to keep her children alive.

Despite my mother's courage and strength, she, like other Cambodian women, was expected to abide by the traditional gender roles that are central to the culture. Women are supposed to marry early and remain in subservient, care-giving roles. In Cambodia, girls are usually married between the ages of sixteen and twenty-five, but sometimes even younger. It is also typical for the groom to be older than the bride by twelve years or more. The Wats, or temples, serve as the religious, cultural, educational, and social centers of the country. Men usually become monks first and then marry after they leave the monastery. The elders make marital decisions and often the groom has some say, but the bride can never go against decisions made for her. My mother always said she never had a choice in her marriage. . . .

Child Labor and Low Prospects

I was eight years old when I began doing full-time manual labor during the time I was not in school. Beginning from second grade, I spent all my summers working on my brother's ten-acre farm located in the "blueberry capital" of Hammonton, New Jersey. It was a family business but the profit never surpassed the effort that we put in. It was such hard work. My brother still owns the farm today, and I go whenever I can for good, grinding exercise. I hoed the ground ten hours a day, from seven a.m. to five p.m. When the summer ended, my mom worked in factories. I accompanied her and stood in the same production lines every weekend and every day when school was not in session. We earned $4.50 an hour under the table working in both freezing cold and sweltering hot factories. To date, I have worked in more than ten different factories at jobs ranging from packaging foods, assembling products, and breaking boxes, to paper and dry cleaning operations. Some days when school ended at three o'clock, I ran home to get on the van and go to work with my mom; we often labored two or more shifts. This experience not only forced me to be an adult at an early age but it also did much harm to my health and my body.

On the farms, as I hoed the ground with my parents, I knew I did not belong there. I felt so hopeless standing out on the field, in the scorching sunlight. But when you are a child, you do what you are told and feel obligated to help your parents. I often asked them what they would do differently if given the opportunity. My dad said if he could go to college, he would study agriculture because farming was all he had known and he loved it. My mom screamed, "No! If I had a chance to go to school, I would become a doctor. I would not be working in blood and sweat with my daughter here in the burning sun. I will make a better life for my children and myself." Standing at four feet, nine inches tall, and weighing only

105 pounds, my mother may not have heard of the word *feminism* and may not understand its meaning, but she exemplifies woman power. . . .

Female Ambition

Throughout high school, I was very active in my community and school. I participated in science fairs and competed in oratorical and art contests. I learned that competition does not just involve winning and losing; it builds leadership and the foundations of self-learning. I was engaged in student government, which gave me experience conducting school fundraisers and food, clothing, and toy drives for the local homeless shelter. Mobilizing my classmates to get involved with their community taught me leadership skills at an early age. A student representative to the Camden City Board of Education my senior year, I had the opportunity to interact with board members and the Superintendent of Schools. I was curious about almost every subject at school, but science, especially medicine and healthcare, interested me the most.

Identifying as a Feminist

When I first came to college, I felt nervous, scared, and eager all at once because I had not seen much of the world outside of Camden City, and yes, I was embarking on something that wasn't expected of a Cambodian girl. . . .

I had never heard of the word *feminism* and never knew there was a major called women's studies until I went to college and took an introductory women's and gender studies course. I used to consider feminism a negative or bad thing because I did not know what it meant, but when I realized it was associated with women's rights, I began to identify as a feminist. There is no set definition of feminism. Naming yourself a feminist and claiming your own understanding of what it means makes you stand out as an individual. When young women discover themselves as feminists and become active leaders, change happens. I believe there is a feminist in every woman across all racial and cultural boundaries, but we do not recognize this because of misconceptions about the term. Although we may have divergent definitions, we are all connected in the pursuit of obtaining gender equality and bettering the lives of women and children. My older sister and I often have long talks about women's issues, and when we get to the word *feminism*, she always makes this statement: "If you are a woman and you believe in your rights as a woman, then you are a feminist!"

During my fifth semester at college, I took a course on feminism, poverty, and public policy. On the first day of class, the professor asked; "What is poverty and with what do you think it is associated?" That was when I sank a little lower into my chair. She said she wanted everyone in the room to introduce themselves and share their thoughts on poverty. At that point, my heart was racing and my palms were wet. The question about poverty terrified me because I had so many answers from personal experience. This course, as well as others I took in women's studies allowed me to reflect on my life experiences and to analyze them in relation to larger social structures, including race, gender, and class, as well as welfare and immigration policies. Women's studies also encouraged me to see a connection between the classroom and the community.

Taking Action to Help Women

One of my greatest experiences at college was being a scholar at the Institute for Women's Leadership, which gave me the opportunity to create such interventions and to exercise my skills as a young woman leader. The program exceeded my expectations: I had the chance to meet and work with remarkable, smart, funny, talented, and committed young women. Their passion and convictions will have a lasting impact on me; when I think of them I smile because I know they are out there causing trouble to make our lives better. I met friends and mentors through the program.

Through an internship and a social action project, I have grown and healed and become a better leader. During my first year in the program, I interned at the Eric B. Chandler Health Center, a federally funded clinic located in New Brunswick, New Jersey, where I worked on projects to support teen mothers, parenting education, domestic violence support groups, prescription assistance, and a self-esteem workshop for patients. As I sat in the office of a social worker at the center, listened to the patients' stories, and participated in the support groups, I felt empowered and moved to help. . . .

Cultural Oppression of Women

If someone were to tell my relatives eleven years ago that one day Rosanna and her sisters would be college graduates and feminists, their jaws would have dropped, thinking it was impossible for these three Cambodian girls to get that far. Although times have changed, many of my relatives still believe that Cambodian women should be obedient, subservient, and dependent on men. For some reason, my mother never fully accepted this ideology, and she taught us something more. She does not want her daughters to live the life that she has lived. She has worked nights, weekends, and double and triple shifts at two to three different jobs at a time to make sure there was food on the table and a shelter over our heads. My mother is a great woman, and she is the force that has kept the family alive. Still, she straddles the old world and the new. She defends the tradition of arranged marriages at the same time that she believes women should have choices and be given the same opportunities as men. When Hillary Clinton ran for president of the United States in the 2008 election, my mom said to her sister, "See, in the U.S., who says a woman can't do the same things as a man?"

It has been hard growing up and it will be challenging to slowly change the cultural beliefs about gender that seemed once to be written in stone. It is difficult to change certain attitudes when so many Cambodians, especially women, accept them. To end this cycle, women must adopt leading, decision-making roles in both the home and the workplace. My mother has taught us that when women are able to define their rights and embrace the feminist within, they will lead by example. This is what my sisters and I are doing. We have all grown up to be like our mother: we refuse to conform and we are throwing gender roles out the window.

Achieving Selfhood

As a recent college graduate with a bachelor of science degree in public health, my career objective is still to become a physician in Camden City, New Jersey, and help improve the health and well-being of women and children living there. I am currently a student at the Ohio University College of Osteopathic Medicine, working toward this long-held goal. I find that every day is an opportunity to learn new things, to try to forgive, and to understand that our past does not dictate who we are. Our past does not make us weaker but pushes us to be stronger, and to further define ourselves and realize our rights as women. I am now a quarter century old and I have found my own definitions, voice, and path in life. My experiences of poverty, abuse, and child labor have left me marked in many ways. But my mother's example of courage, strength, and resilience inspires me. After surviving war, genocide, starvation, hunger, abuse, injustice, gender violence, discrimination, hatred, and extreme poverty, she continues to fight for her daughters. My sisters and I have inherited her will and we will continue her legacy.

The Case Against Marriage

Jessica Bennett and Jesse Ellison

Jessica Bennett is an award-winning senior writer at Newsweek *magazine. She has written on a wide range of topics, including inequality and sexism at work. Jesse Ellison is an articles editor at* Newsweek *and coauthors with Bennett the blog* The Equality Myth.

Bennett and Ellison argue in this article that marriage in the United States is in ruins. The United States has the highest divorce rate in the Western world, and many of the reasons for marriage have vanished. Two-thirds of the breadwinners and co-breadwinners are now women, and unmarried couples have gained legal rights. Moreover, many marriages are just not working, they say. Women today do not choose mates for economic support. Instead, both men and women are looking for "soul mates."

Every year around this time [June], the envelopes begin to arrive. Embossed curlicues on thick-stock, cream-colored paper ask for "the pleasure of our company" at "the union of," "the celebration of," or "the wedding of." With every spring, our sighs get a little deeper as we anticipate another summer of rote ceremony, cocktail hour, and, finally, awkward dancing. Sure, some weddings are fun, but too often they're a formulaic, overpriced, fraught rite of passage marking entry into an institution that sociologists describe as "broken."

Marriage No Longer a Necessity

Once upon a time, marriage made sense. It was how women ensured their financial security, got the fathers of their children to stick around, and gained access to a host of legal rights. But 40 years after the feminist movement established our rights in the workplace, a generation after the divorce rate peaked, and a decade after *Sex and the City* made singledom chic, marriage is—from a legal and practical standpoint, at least—no longer necessary. The two of us are educated, young, urban professionals, committed to our careers, friendships, and, yes, relationships. But we know that legally tying down those unions won't make or break them. Women now constitute a majority of the workforce; we're more educated, less religious, and living longer, with vacuum cleaners and washing machines to make domestic life easier. We're also the breadwinners (or co-breadwinners) in two thirds of American families. In 2010 we know most spousal rights can be easily established outside of the law, and that Americans are cohabiting, happily, in record numbers. We have our own health care and 401(k)s and no longer need a marriage license to visit our partners in the hospital. For many of us, marriage doesn't even mean a tax break.

Evidence That Marriage Is in Ruins

The numbers are familiar but staggering: Americans have the highest divorce rate in the Western world; as many as 60 percent of men and half of women will have sex with somebody other than their spouse during their marriage. . . . So when conservatives argue that same-sex couples are going to "destroy" the "sanctity" of marriage, we wonder, *wait, didn't we already do that?* "Social science tells us fundamentally that this system is not working," says Curtis Bergstrand, a sociologist at Bellarmine University in Louisville, Ky., who has written on marriage. Having donned our share of bridesmaid's dresses, and toasted dozens of nuptials, we'll take reason over romance. Happily ever after doesn't have to include "I do."

Decline in Marriages

Before we get into specifics, a caveat: check with us again in five years. We're in our late 20s and early 30s, right around the time when biological clocks start ticking and whispers of "Why don't you just settle down?" get louder.... So just as *Newsweek* will never live down its (false) prediction that 40-year-old single women were more likely to be "killed by a terrorist" than to marry, we permit you, friends and readers, to mock us at our own weddings (should they happen). Current data may not yet identify our feelings as a so-called trend, but they certainly show we're on to something: the percentage of married Americans has dropped each decade since the 1950s, and the number of unmarried-but-cohabiting partners has risen 1,000 percent over the last 40 years. At 28 for men and 26 for women, the median age at which Americans are marrying is at its highest point ever—and even higher among our cohort of urban and educated. Turns out that waiting is a good idea: for every year we put off marriage, our chances of divorce go down.

No Rationale for Marriage

Which brings us to this question: if you're going to wait, why do it at all? Like a fifth of young Americans, we identify as secular. We know that having children out of wedlock lost its stigma a long time ago: in 2008, 41 percent of births were to unmarried mothers, more than ever before, according to a Pew study. (Older, educated mothers make up the fastest-growing percentage of those births.) And the idea that we'd "save ourselves" for marriage? Please. As one 28-year-old man told the author of a new book on marriage: "If I had to be married to have sex, I would probably be married, as would every guy I know." Even the legal argument for tying the knot is easily debunked. Thanks largely to the efforts of same-sex-marriage advocates, heterosexual couples have more unmarried rights to partnership now than ever. And for the rights we don't have—well, "if you have enough money," says Jennifer Pizer, a senior attorney at the Lambda Legal Defense and Education Fund, "you can pay lawyers to litigate just about anything." To put the icing on the cake, it often pays to stay single: federal law favors unmarried taxpayers in almost every case—only those whose incomes are wildly unequal get a real tax break—and under President [Barack] Obama's new health plan, low-earning single people get better subsidies to buy insurance. As Diana Furchtgott-Roth, writing for the Hudson Institute, put it, "Goodbye, marriage." As of 2013, "unwed Americans may find it even more advantageous—financially, anyway—to stay single."

Changes in the Institution of Marriage

To tell you what you already know, the American family is in the throes of change. Gone are the days of the nuclear nest; in its wake is a motley mix of single parents, same-sex couples, and, yes, unmarried monogamists. Anthropologist Helen Fisher, who studies the nature of love, might say that's a symptom of our biology: she believes humans aren't meant to be together forever, but in short-term, monogamous relationships of three or four years. For us, it's not that we reject monogamy altogether—indeed, one of us is going on six years with a partner—but that the idea of marriage has become so tainted, and simultaneously so idealized, that we're hesitant to engage in it. Boomers may have been the first children of divorce, but ours is a generation for whom multiple households were the norm. We grew up shepherded between bedrooms, minivans, and dinner tables, with step-parents, half-siblings, and highly complicated holiday schedules. You can imagine, then—amid incessant high-profile adultery scandals—that we'd be somewhat cynical about the institution. (Till death do us part, *really*?) "The question," says Andrew Cherlin, the author of *The Marriage-Go-Round*, "is not why fewer people are getting married, but why are so many still getting married?"

Subservience

The feminist argument against marriage has long been that it forces women to conform—as [feminist] Gloria Steinem once

Due to the growing education and compensation in the workplace, women no longer need to marry for financial stability. © Helen King/Corbis.

put it, marriage is an arrangement "for one and a half people." No woman we know would date a man who'd force her into the kitchen—and even Steinem eventually got hitched—but we'd be fools to think we've completely shed the roles associated with "husband" and "wife." Men's contributions to housework and child rearing may have doubled since the 1960s, yet even among dual-earning couples, women still do about two thirds of the housework. (One study even claims that the simple act of getting married creates seven hours more housework for women each week.) In the workplace, meanwhile, women who use their partner's name are regarded as less intelligent, less competent, less ambitious, and thus less likely to be hired. We may date the most modern men in the world, but we've heard enough complaints to worry: if we tie the knot, does life suddenly become a maze of TV dinners, shoes up on the coffee table, and dirty dishes? "The bottom line is that men, not women, are much happier when they're married," says Philip Cohen, a sociologist at the University of North Carolina who studies marriage and family.

Since the early 1900s, the driving force behind marriage, along with procreation, was that women couldn't land well-paying jobs: we relied on our husbands to survive. As recently as 1967, two thirds of female college students (versus 5 percent of men) said they would marry somebody they didn't love if he met their other criteria—primarily, the ability to support them financially. But today, we no longer need to "marry up": women are more educated (we make up nearly 60 percent of college graduates) and better compensated (urban women in their 20s actually outearn their male peers). We are also the so-called entitled generation, brought up with lofty expectations of an egalitarian adulthood; told by helicopter parents and the media, from the moment we exited the womb, that we could be "whatever we wanted"—with infinite opportunities to accomplish those dreams. So you can imagine how, 25 years down the line, committing to another person—*for life*—would be nerve-racking. (How do you know you've found "the one" if you haven't vetted all the options?)

Marry Out of Love, Not Necessity

When we do tie the knot, we do it for love. Young people today don't want their parents' marriage, says Tara Parker-Pope, the author of *For Better*—they want all-encompassing, head-over-heels fulfillment: a best friend, a business partner, somebody to share sex, love, and chores. In other words, a "soulmate"—which is what 94 percent of singles in their 20s describe what they look for in a partner. Yet the idea of a "soulmate" is still a pretty new concept in our romantic history—and one that's hard to maintain. Measurements of brain activity have shown that 20 years into marriage, 90 percent of couples have lost the passion they originally felt. And while couples who marry for love are less "in love" with each passing year, one study found that those in arranged marriages grow steadily more in love as the years progress—because their expectations, say researchers, are a whole lot lower.

Independence

So while little girls may still dream of Prince Charming, they'll be more likely to keep him if they don't expect too much. Research shows that the more education and financial independence a woman has—in other words, the more success she has outside the home—the more likely she is to stay married. (In states where fewer wives have paid jobs, for example, divorce rates tend to be higher.) But when these egalitarian, independent couples decide not to marry at all, they lose none of that stability. Just take a look at couples in Europe: they're happier, less religious, and more likely to believe that marriage is an outdated institution, and their divorce rate is a fraction of our own. . . .

The decline of marriage "doesn't have to spell catastrophe," says Stephanie Coontz, the author of *Marriage, a History.* "We can make marriages better and make nonmarriages work as well."

It may counter what we grew up thinking, but maybe that's not such a bad thing. With our life expectancy in the high 70s, the idea that we're meant to be together forever is less realistic. As Hannah Seligson, the author of *A Little Bit Married*, puts it, there's a "new weight to the words 'I do.'" Healthy partnerships are possible, for sure—but the permanence of marriage seems naive, almost arrogant. "Committing to one person forever is a long time," says Helen Fisher. "I wonder how many people really think about that." If you're anything like us, you'll have plenty of time to do just that— while you're sitting in the pews, at other people's weddings.

A Matriarchal Society
Is Not Imminent

Katha Pollitt

Katha Pollitt is a regular editorialist for the Nation, *a weekly magazine.*

The following viewpoint, Pollitt's editorial in the Nation, *was prompted by Hanna Rosin's essay in the* Atlantic Monthly *titled "The End of Men," about the coming matriarchy throughout the world. Pollitt concedes that for some time women have been completing their educations, entering professions, and generally gaining independence, but, she argues, societies are far from becoming matriarchies. Though women have made progress, men still dominate science and technology and make more money than women do doing the same jobs.*

Don't worry, gentlemen. "The End of Men," Hanna Rosin's much discussed *Atlantic* cover story, isn't really about the end of men. It's about men's declining economic ability to dominate women and various sociocultural consequences of that fact—but who'd read a piece with an unsensational message like that?

We Are Not a Matriarchy

Women are surging forward educationally, entering the professions and the burgeoning service fields in great numbers, having children on their own, putting up with less crap from boyfriends and husbands—we all know that. Men are taking less than half the BAs, have suffered from the decline of manufacturing and other traditionally male jobs, and have lost some of their domestic privileges and some of their cultural prestige—we all know that too. It may even be, as Rosin claims, that women are particularly well suited to the postindustrial economy, where brains, self-discipline, the ability to work well with others and verbal skills matter more than brawn and testosterone-fueled thrill-seeking. It takes a clever picker of statistical and anecdotal cherries, though, to make plausible Rosin's claim that we are on the verge of becoming a matriarchy.

A Preference for Sons Is on the Wane

Take, for example, Rosin's opening vignette. In the 1970s, when flamboyant Marlboro Man biologist Ronald Ericsson figured out how to sort sperm to select a baby's sex, he assumed prospective parents would want boys and was criticized by some feminists for enabling this "universal" desire. Since the 1990s the decision has been made by the woman and to Ericsson's surprise, the majority have gone for girls. "These mothers look at their lives," she writes, "and think their daughters will have a bright future their mother and grandmother didn't have, brighter than their sons, even, so why wouldn't you choose a girl?" Let's cheer that son-preference is on the wane in the United States (but note that a disturbing study shows that men are more likely to stay in a marriage when they have a son, and, as Echidne of the Snakes points out on her blog, a 2007 Gallup poll still gives boys the edge). But it is hardly "over" in South Korea, as Rosin claims; sex-selective abortion is still common there and may be increasing in China, India and Vietnam, as ultrasound becomes more available and prosperity rises. Furthermore, even if those countries' preference for boys vanishes forever while you are reading these words, they will be dealing with the female-unfriendly consequences—including the sale, kidnapping and enslavement of girls and women—for decades.

Men Still Dominate Some Fields

One problem with Rosin's optimistic picture is that every fact she cites in support needs about a dozen asterisks after it:

women may be taking more than half of college degrees, for example, but both men and women are going to college in greater numbers than in previous decades; men still dominate in science, math, engineering and IT [information technology] (where the good jobs are); women need a college degree to earn as much as a man with a high school diploma and, in any case, are sandbagged in the workforce by discrimination, as well as by childcare and eldercare responsibilities men are able, still, to slough off onto their wives or sisters. That women earn 20 to 30 percent less than men in nearly every occupation from salesclerk to surgeon is not a detail, and suggests that gender reversal is hardly around the corner, no matter how well girls do in school.

Many Educated Women Choose Homemaking

Similarly, I'm wary of reading too much into Rosin's interviews with Victoria, Erin and Michelle, sorority sisters at the University of Missouri, Kansas City. These young women are hopeful, organized and ambitious, and assume their lackadaisical boyfriends will be the ones who stay home with the kids. (That would indeed be a role reversal—right now, there are 158,000 stay-home dads, as against 5.1 million stay-home moms.) Great news—does that mean I can throw away my file of articles claiming that startling numbers of young, educated women just want to be homemakers? Or has Rosin, like [New York Times family-life writer] Lisa Belkin before her, found interviewees who illustrate her preconceived ideas? ...

Men Refuse "Women's" Jobs

Must women's gain be men's loss? Her villain isn't feminism but the impersonal workings of postindustrial capitalism, which have marginalized working-class men. But as her title suggests, she sees gender as a zero-sum game. Deprived of the economic superiority that was the basis of their dominance, men don't know what to do with themselves. As Kansas City teacher and social worker Mustafaa El Scari tells the down-and-out deadbeat dads in his fathering class, "All you are is a paycheck, and now you ain't even that: And if you try to exercise your authority, she'll call 911." Excuse me, exercise your authority? Are men really so brittle that they can't imagine a more fluid, flexible, loving, egalitarian way of relating to women and children than "because I said so"? Can they really not take advantage of the expansion of female-dominated working-class jobs like nursing and food preparation? (Actually, aren't most restaurant cooks already men? And if nursing sounds too girly, how about physician's assistant, EMS tech, phlebotomist?) Why should it be that women can change but men cannot?

Boys, Like Girls, Need to Study and Plan

Perhaps boys just haven't had enough incentive. The old ways worked so well for so long, so much of life was rigged in men's favor: all they had to do was show up. It can take a few generations for the new reality to sink in: Unfortunately, society at large isn't doing much to help. American males are bathed from birth in pop culture that reveres the most childish, most retrograde, most narcissistic male fantasies, from misogynistic rap to moronic action movies. Where would they get the idea that they should put away the video game and do their homework? That social work or schoolteaching is a good life for a man? Girls get a ton of sexist messages, too. But even if they grow up hating their bodies and dressing like prostitutes, they know that if they don't want to end up waitressing, they got to hit the books and make a plan.

Hit the books. Make a plan. Boys can do that.

Women Must Take Ownership of Their Finances

Suze Orman

Suze Orman is an author, TV personality, and columnist specializing in personal finance.

Jane Eyre's literal independence is made possible by the fortune she inherits from her relatives. In the following article, Orman examines women's relationship to their money. She says that women should value and manage their money because it enables those things women value most in life. Women have made fabulous leaps in the business and professional worlds, but they lack confidence and interest in their personal finances. And without wise control of their personal finances, they can never be truly independent. There is, she contends, a "universal block . . . preventing women from being as powerful as they are meant to be." Orman has learned from older women that their regrets about not taking charge of their financial lives, is a failure that leaves them feeling "powerless" and "worthless." As callous as it sounds, she writes, nothing affects happiness more than money.

Women today make up nearly half of the total workforce in this country. Over the past thirty years, women's income has soared a dramatic 63 percent. Fifty-one percent of all professional- and managerial-level workers are women. Women bring in half or more of the income in the majority of U.S. households—a growing trend that made the cover of *Newsweek* and was front-page news in many of the nation's newspapers. Women-owned businesses comprise 40 percent of all companies in the United States. There are more women than ever before who can count themselves among the country's millionaires, more women in upper management, and more women in positions of power in the government.

We have a right to be proud of our progress. I am so honored to witness this revolution in my lifetime. I only wish it told the whole truth.

Ignorant of Money

Now, would you like to hear the other side of the story? Ninety percent of women who participated in a 2006 survey commissioned by Allianz Insurance rated themselves as feeling insecure when it came to their finances. *Ninety* percent! In the same survey, *nearly half* the respondents said that the prospect of ending up a bag lady has crossed their minds. A 2006 Prudential financial poll found that only 1 percent of the women surveyed gave themselves an A in rating their knowledge of financial products and services. Two-thirds of women have not talked with their husbands about such things as life insurance and preparing a will. Nearly 80 percent of women said they would depend on Social Security in their golden years. Did you know that women are nearly twice as likely as men to retire in poverty? . . .

In 1980, when I was hired as a financial advisor for Merrill Lynch, I was one of the few women in the Oakland, California, office. In the eyes of my (male) boss, that made me the perfect candidate to work with all the women who walked through the door. . . . No matter the circumstances that brought them to the brokerage firm, they all had the same reason for being there: They did not want the responsibility of managing their money. I always felt they hired me simply to babysit their money for them.

Disinclined to Take Responsibility for Money

More than thirty years later, the story is much the same. Regardless of the gains in our financial status, I know and you know that women still don't want to take responsibility when it comes to their money. Yes, women are making more money than ever before, but they are not making more of what they make. What do I mean by that? Your retirement money sits in cash because you haven't figured out how to invest it properly, so you do nothing. . . .

Giving Up Power

It's about how you berate yourself all the time for not knowing more and doing more . . . yet stay resigned to this feeling of helplessness and despair as time ticks away.

This problem, in my opinion, is enormous and pervasive and universal. It crosses all ages, all races, all tax brackets. Who can deny the fact that there is a fundamental block at work here that is preventing women from becoming as powerful as they are meant to be? Not me. I would be the first one to tell you that everything you need to know to secure your financial future, to educate yourself, to make your life easy— it's all out there. Yours for the asking. But you don't ask; you don't want to know.

I see this fundamental denial, this resistance in all women, no matter what they do, how they live, or where they are in their lives. I see you literally giving your money away rather than dealing with it. I see stay-at-home moms who work twenty-four hours a day and yet hand over all power and control to their husbands because they don't earn the money. I see successful single women who refuse to focus on what they need to do today to ensure their financial security years from now. I see women in second marriages who fail to protect the assets they accumulated before they remarried and feel uncomfortable bringing up money issues with their new husbands. I see divorced women of all ages who go into full-blown panic mode when faced with the reality that they have no clue what money exists, what to do when they get their share of the settlement, and whether they will be able to main-

According to Orman, women should take control over their finances. © Andrew Brookes/ Corbis.

tain their lifestyle post-divorce. And the most heartbreaking of them all? I hear older women use words like "powerless" and "worthless" to describe themselves. These women are filled with regret when it comes to the way they've lived their financial lives.

So why do you all do this to yourselves? Why are you voluntarily committing financial suicide, and doing it with a smile on your face?

Competent in Every Way but Financially

Let me put it another way. Ask yourself this:

Why is it that women, who are so competent in all other areas of their lives, cannot find the same competence when it comes to matters of money?

I have asked this question—of myself and others—over and over. Of course, there is no one answer. After much contemplation, here is what I have come up with:

The matter of women and money is clearly a complicated issue that has much to do with our history and traditions, both societal and familial. These deep-seated issues are major hurdles to overcome, major tides to turn—and that doesn't happen overnight. It can take generations to effect change of this magnitude in our daily behavior. . . . They are absolutely a root cause of this problem. . . . [But we] have to look at this on a behavioral level, too, since traits that are fundamental to our nature clearly affect how we approach money as well.

Consider this: It's a generally accepted belief that nurturing comes as a basic instinct to women. We give of ourselves; we take care of our family, our friends, our colleagues. It's in our nature to nurture. So why don't we take care of our money? Why don't we want to take care of our money as well as we take care of the spouses, partners, children, pets, plants, and whatever else is in our lives that we love and cherish?

Women Need a Relationship with Money

I want you to think about that question. The answer is critical to uncovering what is at work here and what is holding you back. So I'll ask it again:

Why don't we show our money the same care and attention that we shower on every other important relationship in our lives?

Because we don't have a relationship with our money.

Correction: We do have a relationship with our money. It's just a totally dysfunctional one.

Let me tell you why I say this. Across the board, I see women refusing to engage with their money until they are forced to—because of the birth of children, or divorce, or death, for example. In other words, we do not relate to it until we are in extreme, life-changing situations in which we have no choice but to confront money matters. Until then, we don't apply that same primal, nurturing impulse when it comes to taking care of our money—and by extension, *ourselves*. We can't even accept this as a fact—that our money is indeed an extension of ourselves. Instead, we persist in a dysfunctional relationship—we ignore our money, deny its needs, we are afraid of it, afraid of failing, afraid it will expose our short-comings, which leads to shame. What do we do with all these uncomfortable feelings? We suppress them, we put them away, we don't deal with them. It becomes far easier to ignore the money issue altogether. And the longer we ignore it, the worse the situation becomes; we grow even more fearful as time passes that it's too late for us to learn, too late to even try. So we give up. Who likes a failed relationship? Nobody. Better to have no relationship at all than a failed one. . . .

Money and Happiness

Now let's talk about happiness for a moment.

The simple fact is that nothing more directly affects your happiness than money.

Oh, I know, some of you are just horrified by this notion, maybe even offended. *Suze, how could you?!* Happiness is about all the things money can't buy—health, love, respect—right? Absolutely true—all of these are essential to a happy life. All are determined by who you are and not what you have. But the kind of happiness I am talking about is your quality of life—the ability to enjoy life, to live life to its fullest potential. And I challenge anyone to tell me that such things aren't factors in your overall happiness.

Let's just walk through this together for a moment. Yes, I know that your health and the health of your loved ones is paramount, but explain to me what would happen if, God forbid, any one of you fell ill. Wouldn't you want the best care that money can buy? Wouldn't you be grateful that you were in a good health plan? And isn't it money that puts the roof over your head, and money that allows you to move to a neighborhood with a great public school system? And money that allows you to retire early, or quit your job while you go back to school to pursue a new career?

For Further Discussion

1. Discuss the autobiographical aspects of *Jane Eyre*, citing from the selections by Rosengarten and Gaskell.

2. How would you assess Jane's view of organized religion and the clergy in her journey toward independence? How would you describe the religion she finally comes to accept? See the selections by Ewbank, Blom, and Pell for help.

3. Discuss the parallels between British colonialism and woman's dependency as it unfolds in Jane's life. See especially the selections by Meyer and Zonana.

4. Outline the critical argument over whether Jane can have both love and independence. What is your opinion? Cite from the selections in the text in your answer.

5. Is Jane a social rebel? If so, in what sense? If not, why not? See the selections by Eagleton, Pollitt, Orman, and Pell for help with your answer.

6. Discuss the state of domesticity and woman's independence in the contemporary world, citing from Eang, Bennett and Ellison, Pollitt, and Orman.

For Further Reading

Jane Austen, *Emma*. 1815.

————, *Pride and Prejudice*. 1813.

Anne Brontë, *Agnes Grey*. 1849.

Charlotte Brontë, *The Professor: A Tale*. 1857.

————, *Shirley: A Tale*. 1847.

————, *Villette*. 1853.

Emily Brontë, *Wuthering Heights*. 1847.

George Eliot, *Middlemarch*. 1874.

Elizabeth Gaskell, *Mary Barton: A Tale of Manchester Life*. 1848.

Bibliography

Books

Nancy Armstrong   *Desire and Domestic Fiction: A Political History of the Novel.* New York: Oxford University Press, 1987.

K.D. Arnold   *Lives of Promise: What Becomes of High School Valedictorians.* San Francisco: Jossey-Bass, 1994.

Harriet Bjork   *The Language of Truth: Charlotte Brontë, the Woman Question, and the Novel.* Lund, Sweden: Gleerup, 1974.

Kathleen Blake   *Love and the Woman Question in Victorian Literature: The Art of Self-Postponement.* Brighton, UK: Harvester, 1983.

Rosemarie Bodenheimer   *The Politics of Story in Victorian Social Fiction.* Ithaca, NY: Cornell University Press, 1988.

Penny Boumelha   *Charlotte Brontë.* Bloomington: Indiana University Press, 1990.

Charles Burkhart   *Charlotte Brontë A Psychosexual Study of Her Novels.* London: Gollancz, 1973.

David Deirdre   *Rule Britannia: Women, Empire and Victorian Writing.* Ithaca, NY: Cornell University Press, 1995.

Sandra M. Gilbert and Susan Gubar — *The Madwoman in the Attic. The Woman Writer and the Nineteenth-Century Literary Imagination.* New Haven, CT: Yale University Press, 1979.

Arlie Russell Hochschild — *The Second Shift.* New York: Penguin, 2003.

Robert Bernard Martin — *Accents of Persuasion: Charlotte Brontë's Novels.* London: Faber, 1966.

Helene Moglen — *Charlotte Brontë: The Self Conceived.* New York: Abacus, 1971.

Margot Peters — *The Unquiet Soul: A Biography of Charlotte Brontë.* London: Hodder and Stoughton, 1975.

Mary Poovey — *Uneven Developments: The Ideological Work of Gender in Mid-Victorian England.* London: Virago, 1989.

Elaine Showalter — *A Literature of Their Own: British Women Novelists from Brontë to Lessing.* Princeton, NJ: Princeton University Press, 1977.

Alice Steinback — *Without Reservations. The Travels of an Independent Woman.* New York: Random House, 2000.

Sarah Weddington — *A Question of Choice.* New York: Penguin, 1993.

T.J. Wise and J.A. Symington, eds. — *The Brontës: Their Lives, Friendships and Correspondence.* 4 vols. 1933. Oxford: Basil Blackwell, 1980.

Periodicals

H.D. Bernard et al.	"A Residue of Tradition," *Journal of Marriage and the Family*, vol. 49, 1987.
Francine Blau	"Trends in the Well-Being of American Women, 1970–1995," *Journal of Economic Literature*, March 1998.
Christa Crosby	"Charlotte Brontë's Haunted Text," *SEL*, vol. 24, 1984.
Peter Allan Dale	"Heretical Narrative: Charlotte Brontë's Search for Endlessness," *Religion and Literature*, vol. 16, 1984.
Susan Diesenhouse	"At Home with Joan and Robert R. Parker; A House Divided, Lovingly," *New York Times*, August 23, 2001.
Laura E. Donaldson	"The Miranda Complex: Colonialism and the Question of Feminist Reading," *Diacritics*, vol. 18, 1988.
Richard Dunn	"The Natural Heart: Jane Eyre's Romanticism," *Wordsworth Circle*, vol. 10, 1979.
R. Victor Fuchs	"Sex Differences in Economic Well Being," *Science*, April 1986.
Mary Ellis Gibson	"The Seraglio or Suttee: Brontë's *Jane Eyre*," *Postscript*, vol. 4, 1987.
Sandra M. Gilbert	"Life's Empty Pack: Notes Toward a Literary Daughteronomy," *Critical Inquiry*, vol. 11, 1985.

Peter Grudin — "Jane and the Other Mrs. Rochester: Excess and Restraint in *Jane Eyre*," *Novel*, vol. 10, 1977.

Franklin J. Jeffrey — "The Merging of Spirituality: Jane Eyre as Missionary of Love," *Nineteenth-Century Literature*, vol. 49, 1995.

Carla Kaplan — "Girl Talk: *Jane Eyre* and the Romance of Woman's Narrative," *Novel*, vol. 30, 1995.

K.C. Kling et al. — "Gender Differences in Self-Esteem: A Meta-Analysis," *Psychological Bulletin*, vol. 125, 1999.

John Kucich — "Passionate Reserve and Reserved Passion in the Works of Charlotte Brontë," *ELH*, vol. 52, 1985.

Hermione Lee — "Emblems and Enigmas in *Jane Eyre*," *English*, vol. 30, 1981.

Caroline Levine — "'Harmless Pleasure': Gender Suspense and *Jane Eyre*," *Victorian Literature and Culture*, vol. 28, 2000.

Anita Levy — "*Jane Eyre*, the Woman Writer, and the History of Experience," *Modern Language Quarterly*, vol. 56, 1995.

Paul Schacht — "Jane Eyre and the History of Self-Respect," *Modern Language Quarterly*, vol. 52, 1991.

Carol Senf — "*Jane Eyre*: The Prison House of Victorian Marriage," *Journal of Women's Studies in Literature*, vol. 1, 1979.

Paula Sullivan — "Fairy Tale Elements in *Jane Eyre*," *Journal of Popular Culture*, vol. 12, 1978.

Moser Thomas — "What Is the Matter with Emily Jane?" *Nineteenth-Century Fiction*, June 1962.

Robert Weiss and Nancy Morse Samuelson — "Social Roles of American Women," *Marriage and Family Living*, November 1985.

Susan Ostrov Weisser — "Charlotte Brontë, Jane Austen, and the Meaning of Love," *Brontë Studies*, July 2006.

L. Wichstrom — "The Emergence of Gender Difference in Depressed Mood During Adolescence," *Developmental Psychology*, vol. 35, 1999.

Index